AVEN'U
BOYS

Frank Pugliese

56 E 81st St., NY NY 10028–0202
212–772–8334/FAX 772–8358

AVEN'U BOYS
© Copyright 1994 by Frank Pugliese

First printing: June 1994
ISBN: 0-88145-114-2

Book design: Marie Donovan
Word processing: Microsoft Word for Windows
Typographic controls: Xerox Ventura Publisher 2.0 PE
Typeface: Palatino
Printed on recycled acid-free paper and bound in the USA.

ABOUT THE AUTHOR

Frank Pugliese, a first-generation Italian immigrant who grew up on the stoops of Brooklyn, is a graduate of NYU Film School and a former Playwright-in-Residence at the Royal Court in London. His play THE SUMMER WINDS was produced at NY Stage and Film. Other short plays, including THE KING OF CONNECTICUT, have been done at Naked Angels, where Frank served as one of the company's first Artistic Directors. Among the many works developed there was AVEN'U BOYS, which Frank will be directing the film version of for Maverick. Other film projects include: DION, a screenplay about Dion and the Belmonts, with Frank to direct and Barry Levinson to produce; a screenplay adaptation of Wendy Riss' play A DARKER PURPOSE called THE WINNER, which Frank will direct; a screenplay detailing the Buddy Boys corruption scandal with Nick Gomez (LAWS OF GRAVITY) to direct; an updated version of OLIVER TWIST for Oliver Stone to direct and Quincy Jones to produce; and MOB GIRL for Rosalie Swedlin at Universal. Most recently, Frank won the WGA award for a script he wrote for the series HOMICIDE.

ORIGINAL PRODUCTIONS

AVEN'U BOYS was originally produced by NAKED ANGELS, opening on the 23 September 1989. The cast and creative contributors were as follows:

WENDY	Marisa Tomei
ANN	Nancy Travis
LINDA	Kasi Lemmons
ED	Patrick Breen
CHARLIE	Fisher Stevens
ROCKY	Rob Morrow
Director	Pippin Parker
Sets	David Hohmann
Lights	Chris Kondek
Costumes	Carmel Dundon
Assistant director	Christie Wagner
Fight choreography	B H Barry

AVEN'U BOYS was subsequently produced by Ron Kastner, William B O'Boyle, Sonny Everett, and Evangeline Morphos at the John Houseman Theater, opening on 8 March 1993. The cast and creative contributors were as follows:

WENDY .... Lili Taylor
ANN .... Lucinda Jenney
LINDA .... Cynthia Martells
ED .... Ron Eldard
CHARLIE .... Michael Imperioli
ROCKY .... Adrian Pasdar

Director .... Frederick Zollo
Sets .... Kert Lundell
Lights .... Jan Kroeze
Costumes .... Carol Oditz
Sound .... John Kilgore
Fight choreography .... B H Barry

DEDICATION

To my parents, who travelled centuries
To the ones who got left behind
To Marisa, my inspiration

ACT ONE

THEN & NOW

PROLOGUE

(The lights come up on the three women)

WENDY: When they were kids the boys sat on the stoop and bull. Bull about ball, girls, gettin' laid that is, and how to get outta school.

ANN: When they were old enough they moved to Rosie's Candy Store on the corner. Best egg creams in Brooklyn. Snatch a piece of Bazooka; have Rosie pull your ear off.

LINDA: When they were old enough they moved to the bar under the tracks.

WENDY: We got 'em outta the bars.

LINDA: The place is Avenue U, in Bensonhurst, in Brooklyn, a borough of New York City. Even though everybody just calls Manhattan "The City". It's otherwise called "Aven-U"—all in one word. The boys hung out on the last corner of Aven-U. A block from Lafayette. And a couple a blocks from the projects.

ANN: Neil Sedaka, Neil Diamond, Barbra Streisand, Buddy Hackett, Sandy Koufax, and others came from around here. A lot of famous people come from Brooklyn.

WENDY: But they're all Jewish. The boys are Italian. From the West Side. From hard-working people who

live in rowhouses and are Catholic—sometimes. They
love to eat, play cards, and fight. They got up to four or
five generations packed into this neighborhood. It's a
tightly wrapped place which makes for a lotta tension....

ANN: I should say Italian American. My father was
from over there. He kept photos of the old country in
a jar. The thing is, in the photos, him and his friends
are always huggin'. Walkin' arm and arm. Even kissin'
each other. Somethin' Italian. Somethin' he hadda give
up over here. He used to say "You gotta be hard in
America."

LINDA: But the boys don't come into the projects
and the projects don't come into the neighborhood.
Nobody really says anything about it, it's just the way
it is. I think they built the things on a swamp, 'cause the
basements are always flooded. And that genius Robert
Moses, he put the El on one side, and the highway on
the other, the train yards in the back. The only street
there is, you look right across and see the neon of the
gelati gardens, pizza, Italian ices, sandwiches. I tell you
that place looks like a picnic most every night. You can
see almost anything, except a black face.

WENDY: Here comes a Frank Sinatra tune I love.
(We hear Sinatra sing a snippet of "What is America
to Me") Sure I like rock but I love Frankie. It's like
a requirement around here.

LINDA: He was handsome.

WENDY: He's still handsome. He's the kinda man I
wanna end up with.

LINDA: The first half of this story, this story, is either
yesterdays or today. It goes all over the places. It's in
pieces. I know, alot a stories are like books. But no story
I know is in a book. They're all in pieces.

WENDY: Everything that takes place out here on
the street is a year ago, the last month of high school.
And everything that takes place back there is like now.

(Blackout)

Scene One
THEN

*(The action in this scene is of primary importance. We open
up with* ED *hitting* CHARLIE *in the shoulder. Then* CHARLIE
hits ED *in the shoulder. They are trading hits. Each punch
is successively harder. One wins when the other is finally
knocked down or loses use of his arm. When one is down, the
third comes in to play.* ROCKY *will come in to play the game
after* CHARLIE *loses. While* CHARLIE *is waiting for his turn,
he should be punching something and looking at his knuckles.
The discussion they have is slow and of secondary importance
to the punching.* ROCKY *is leaning up against the wall.)*

ED: I am the fuckin' strongest son-of-a-bitch in this
neighborhood.

CHARLIE: Who you bull-shittin'? Soon I be the strongest.
(Punch)

ED: Just fuckin' try, you ain't got the nerve to hit me.
Scared I'll twist your face off. *(Punch)*

CHARLIE: Yeah! *(Punch)*

ED: Yeah!

(Punch. ROCKY *steps off the wall and moves forward toward
the audience.)*

ROCKY: Whatta piece a ass! *(Turns around, heads back to
the wall, and puts himself in the same exact pose as before)*
Whatta'm I doin' here?

*(*ED *makes a masturbating gesture.)*

CHARLIE: We shoulda went to Shea.

ROCKY: We should go to the City and hang. Let the sweat cool.

ED: You're playin' the same record over and over.

ROCKY: *(Squeezes his nose shut)* I think I smell chicken shit.

ED: We got everything we need right here. Movies, food, and snatch.

ROCKY: I'm so bored I can't even smile.

ED: Go fuck a hole.

ROCKY: *(Grabs his crotch)* Suck this.

ED: Hey, don't throw it around.

CHARLIE: Keep it in your pants. It stinks.

ED: If it needs some air fan out at the Wrong Number.

(ROCKY *hits the floor and starts doing some push-ups.* ED *tries to catch a fly.)*

ED: Fuckin' fly.

ROCKY: Hey, what happen with that guy?

(CHARLIE *punches.)*

ED: What guy? *(Punch)*

ROCKY: That guy.

CHARLIE: *(Punches)* The nigger.

ED: You mean the fuckin' dumb ass.

ROCKY: Yeah!

ED: Still in the hospital.

CHARLIE: Word is he's gonna live. *(Punch)*

ED: That's a shame. I coulda sworn I killed him with that last punch.

CHARLIE: He raps him in the head with a baseball bat and the guy's still running. *(Punch)*

ED: They ain't human. They come from some African animal or somethin'. *(Punch)*

CHARLIE: I heard his head crack.

ROCKY: Cops all over, I hear.

ED: You know, I don't get it. I mean, I ain't done nothin' wrong. I hit the fuck. He ain't got no right to be here. They belong where they belong and we belong where we belong. And he don't belong near me.

CHARLIE: He was squirmin' on the floor. He was like Curly from the Three Stooges. We ain't got nothin' to worry about, he can't talk. I heard he's gonna be a mental retard.

ROCKY: He was new in the projects.

(CHARLIE *punches* ED.)

ED: Somebody shoulda' told him. They know enough to know he shouldn't come around for no fuckin' sandwich.

ROCKY: He was coming back from a date.

CHARLIE: Got a lot of nerve wearin' a suit in this neighborhood. Well-dressed bastard... Who the hell he think he is? Projects ruined the neighborhood.

ED: I see them all shoppin' down Aven'U and 86th.

CHARLIE: They bombed out the black guy on my block.

ED: She comes runnin' out naked. Looked like *National Geographic.*

CHARLIE: They move in, your house is worth half.

ED: If he stayed on his side of the tracks none of this woulda happened.

(The sounds of a car shooting by)

CHARLIE: Monte Carlo SS.

ED: Monte Carlo? Wipe your eyes you're still sleepin'.

CHARLIE: What wuz that Rock?

ROCKY: Lincoln Continental...Bill Blass Edition.

CHARLIE: In a Continental, them leather seats don't stick to your ass.

ED: Continental is old. A Mustang GT 5.0 is mint.

CHARLIE: How's about you Rocky?

ROCKY: Lamborghini.

ED: Every time you gotta come outta left field.

CHARLIE: Don't you eat lamborghini?

ROCKY: You're guineas and you don't know shit about Italy.

CHARLIE: It's the shape of a bitch's boot.

ED: With a high heel.

CHARLIE: They used to eat lions in Italy. *(Punch)*

ED: Tasted some horse meat from Jersey once.

ROCKY: Charlie, lions used to eat them.

CHARLIE: Fuckin' sick people.

ED: I kept kickin' him in the face, but he don't die! Fuckin' thirty-dollar shoes full of blood. Fuckin' messy bastard. I gotta throw my shoes away. *(Punch)*

CHARLIE: Ed was givin' 'em all them TV wrestlin' moves.

ED: I give him credit for standin' so long. I kept whackin' him with that bat. Fuckin' guy threw up on me, but he still don't go down. *(Punch)*

CHARLIE: *(Buckles with the blow)* Shit!

ED: What's-a-matta Charlie, got you fallin'?

CHARLIE: I ain't fallin' that easy. *(Punch—weak and ineffective)*

ED: I gonna put you away. *(Punch. CHARLIE falls to the floor.)* Gonna get up? Wanna try again?

CHARLIE: Yeah, wait, I ain't down.

ED: *(Gently places his foot on CHARLIE's stomach)* Get up. Go ahead and get up. (CHARLIE *strains but he can't get up.* ED *grabs his crotch.)* Stay down. You're out. Come on, Rock. *(He reaches up and out of the air and grabs the fly. He shakes it in his hand and then slaps his hands together.)* Killed that mother-fuckin' fly.

CHARLIE: *(Looks at* ED*'s hands)* That's no fly, that's a lightning bug. It's a smear a light.

ED: It's green. They're pretty...lightning bugs.

ROCKY: *(Steps up and punches* ED*)* Some a dem black guys from the projects say they gonna come down to bust heads.

ED: The day somebody busts my ass you might as well stick it to yourself 'cause this world's over. *(Punch)*

ROCKY: Projects are real mad. Looks like trouble. *(Punch)*

ED: Project's full of noise. You know how many boys I put away. Fuckin' boys who think they can fight me. *(Punch)*

ROCKY: We should go to Manhattan.

CHARLIE: What? You gonna move to the Island like the rest of them faggots?

ED: I'm a fighter not a runner. *(Punch)*

ROCKY: Check out some pussy.

ED: *(Punches* ROCKY*)* Tired of Brooklyn?

ROCKY: *(Punches* ED*)* Whatta you scared?

ED: Of faggots on white bread?

(He punches ROCKY. CHARLIE *starts punching the sign.)*

ROCKY: What the hell are you doing?

CHARLIE: I'm punchin' the sign.

ROCKY: I know you're punchin' the sign, but what the fuck for?

ED: Charlie, you're fuckin' demented, you know that?

CHARLIE: Fuck up, I know what I'm doin'.

ROCKY: Well, you gonna tell us or you gonna keep it a secret? *(He punches* ED, *who punches him right back.)*

CHARLIE: See, this here supposed to build your knuckles. Makes 'em red, then you get them callous or somethin', you know, hard skin. Then when you hit a nigger you can watch his face split like a watermelon. *(Starts laughing)* A watermelon.

ED: You're a dumb fuck, you know that.

CHARLIE: Why don't I try it on you, big shit.

ED: After I'm finished with Rocky I'm gonna go with you again. Just this time, instead of your arm, I'm gonna punch your face in. *(Punch)*

CHARLIE: Look, I read this in one of them muscle mags.

ED: Dipshit, you want hard knuckles, buy a pair of brass knuckles. You ain't never gonna get yours that hard.

*(*ROCKY *punches* ED.*)*

CHARLIE: I neva thought of that.

ED: Why don't you ask me before you do somethin'?

CHARLIE: I don't know.

ROCKY: And I hang out with these ova-achievas.

ED: *(Punch)* Hurtin', Rock?

ROCKY: I'm fine. *(Punch)* Don't you worry about me.

ED: You're down soon enough.

(He punches hard. ROCKY *takes a step back—he's hurt.)*

CHARLIE: Rock gonna quit this early. Yellow ass.

ROCKY: No chance.

(Steps in and gives a punch. It has no effect on ED.*)*

ED: What was that, a love tap? *(Winds up and punches.* ROCKY *falls to the ground and curls up.)* You're on the floor, coward.

CHARLIE: Get up. Come on, one more shot, Rock. You can do it.

ROCKY: I can't move my fuckin' arm. I can't feel a God-damn thing. It's dead.

CHARLIE: No joke?

ED: Shit, I didn't punch you hard.

ROCKY: I can't move it. Holy Jesus shit, I'm goin' home.

(He starts running as he holds his arm.)

CHARLIE: Hope they don't cut it off.

ED: Don't worry. It's just a little numb, it'll go away. Don't be a fag. Come back.

CHARLIE: Fag.

(ED punches CHARLIE.)

(Overlap to:)

Linda #1

LINDA: Rocky. I met Rocky like a year ago, about. When I got back to Brooklyn, I was never plannin' on stayin' long. But he was such a sweetheart. Deep down he can't even hurt a roach. And you know how ugly they are....

Rocky, he picks me up once. He's more excited than one of my kids. Like his eyes are jumpin' out of his head. He throws me into the back of a borrowed Cadillac. And the next thing I know, I'm walking around the grass and sand on the side of the Belt Parkway looking for a tiger. Rocky tells me, somebody lost their tiger, he jumped out of the car. I ask him: First, why would his friend have a tiger; two, if he did, what's it doin' in the car; and three, what do we do when we find him? That's when Rocky growled and took my shirt off with his teeth....

Maybe it's 'cause he has some brains in 'im. Not like them other two. Those two could smack their heads together and probably wonder who's at the door. He's got something....

(Overlap to:)

Scene Two
NOW

(Lights up on ROCKY. *He is looking at himself in a mirror, which is the audience. He is wearing a suit. He checks his money, face, underarms, underwear.)*

ROCKY: Hey, you wanna hear a tiger's matin' call? "Hey tiger, wanna fuck?"

(Tries the line several different ways)

"Hey tiger, wanna fuck?" "Hey tiger, wanna fuck?" Baby, what's the last thing you do before you go to bed? You pray. Will you pray for me? Will you pray for me? Will you pray for me???

(He straightens his clothes and exits.)

(Overlap to:)

Scene Three
NOW

(Lights up on two bar stools and a bar out front. LINDA *sits on one of the stools, smoking a cigarette. She looks around the place, bored and lonely.* ROCKY *struts by, fixes himself with cocky assurances, and sits down next to her.)*

ROCKY: Hi there.

(She turns. When ROCKY *sees that she's a black woman, he's taken aback.)*

LINDA: 'Bye.

ROCKY: You're.... *(Looks around)* You shouldn't....

LINDA: What?!

ROCKY: The cigarette smoke gets in my eyes.

LINDA: Then move.

ROCKY: *(Stares at her)* I...

LINDA: Whatta you starin' at? You never seen a woman before?

ROCKY: Don't I....

LINDA: Don't even try it, I'm not interested.

ROCKY: Try what?

LINDA: Don't I know you from someplace...you got the time...what's a nice girl like you doing in a place like this...come here often...what's your line, Mister GQ?

ROCKY: Whatta you keep records?...How about wanna fuck?

LINDA: Clever. Original, too... Not one for poetry, are you?

ROCKY: How about wanna screw. Sometimes that works better.

LINDA: Little different, but same idea, right? Look, don't bother, I'm tired.

ROCKY: Oh, am I bothering you.... Hey, I mean, I really don't wanna bother ya.... I'd never wanna bother ya. Ya know that comes from the depths of my heart, don't ya. I really wouldn't wanna bother ya.

LINDA: You're bothering me.

ROCKY: I am bothering you. You know, I was standing there and I said, "Gee. I'm gonna sit there and, golly, I hope I don't bother her."

LINDA: Well Gomer Pyle, you're bothering me.

ROCKY: I don't know. I guess I'm a natural-born bother.

LINDA: I guess.

(A pause as they avoid each other)

ROCKY: Do you know who I am?

LINDA: You're a horny white boy lookin' for his first piece of black ass?

ROCKY: Black? It's dark in here. Are you really black?

LINDA: Yeah! Well I guess I'm really like a brown, mocha, chocolate kinda color.

ROCKY: *(Touches her hand)* Your skin feels like white skin. It's warm like white skin. Why, if I close my eyes....

LINDA: I'm black.

ROCKY: I know.

LINDA: Who the fuck are you?

ROCKY: Hey...hey...I'm famous. The PTA, the church groups, aerobicize classes...no one's told you about me?

LINDA: I'm too busy to play aerobics. I just moved back here.

ROCKY: From where?

LINDA: Manhattan.

ROCKY: New York City?

LINDA: Yeah. The one in the postcards.

ROCKY: Whatta you doin' here?

LINDA: What?! I can't get a drink in this bar? My money is green like yours.

ROCKY: Ding-ding-ding. This round's over, champ.... Whatta you doin' in Brooklyn?

LINDA: Money. Love. When you don't get 'em ya move to Brooklyn.

ROCKY: Whatta ya do in the city?

LINDA: First college. Then the boy. Then the girl. Then he leaves. Then I leave. You in school?

ROCKY: Out a few years. But I graduated.

LINDA: I mean college.

ROCKY: I went to work.

LINDA: Doing what?

ROCKY: Actually, I came in for a little drink. Take a little break from my work.

LINDA: What kinda work?

ROCKY: Oh, I'm a nuclear scientist you might say. Yeah...I build them little bombs that blow you and me up. Give me a rush just thinkin' about the explosion. The giant mushroom, the tremors, the explosion. Beautiful, don't cha think? Don't it give you a rush?

LINDA: *(Laughs)* Where do you do this work?

ROCKY: Got a little bomb laboratory a couple of blocks from here.

LINDA: I suppose you wanna show me one.

ROCKY: Don't wanna be a bother.

LINDA: No bother.

ROCKY: Since I was a kid I've been obsessed with the atom. Me and the atom bomb, we're buddies. It's my best friend.

LINDA: You make a living off of this?

ROCKY: I live.... Listen to the experiment. You're Russia, you know, the old one, and I'm the bomb. I attack, invade, then bang the world ends.... Romantic, ain't it?

LINDA: Romantic, I don't know. How much one a these bombs cost somebody like me.

ROCKY: Why don't you make me breakfast.

LINDA: The post-nuclear breakfast in bed?

ROCKY: Everything microwaved.

LINDA: I make some mean eggs.

ROCKY: It's bigger than Nagasaki.

LINDA: I can't, I got two kids to feed come breakfast.

ROCKY: Make me a cup of coffee.

LINDA: *(Pause)* It'll blow you away.

(They get up.)

ROCKY: I'll meet you outside.

LINDA: All...right...

ROCKY: No. I...I gotta pee.

LINDA: No, I understand.

ROCKY: Nah, I really gotta pee.

LINDA: So I can wait.

ROCKY: Nah, it's cool. It's stuffy in here. Please. Outside.

LINDA: You'll fuck me. But you won't walk out a bar with me.

ROCKY: *(Looks around)* Shit... *(Grabs her hand and walks out)* I'll pee later.

(Overlap to:)

Linda #2

LINDA: Tough guys. I have known tough guys. Guys so handsome girls stayed away. But I didn't. I thought I was tough too. Tough as leather. But leather don't keep you warm for shit. I was so tough I went to the city. But I don't eat my salad with the right fork. And I never had enough for a taxi. And I always got into places when there was nobody in 'em. And I always got the wrong haircut. And I always bought last year's clothes on sale. And I always felt like I was tryin' to catch up on somethin'. Somethin', I don't even know what....

I married a doorman. He wore a uniform. That's supposed to be sexy. I thought it made him serious. He got tipped for bein' polite, for smilin'. I took politeness for romance, and smilin' for personality. He was tough. And I was smart. Yeah, I was so smart I went to college.

But I wasn't smart enough to walk out the door on a doorman....

(Overlap to:)

Scene Four
NOW

(Lights up on ED *and* ANN *in bed.* ED *bolts up, clutching his pillow.* ANN *slowly wakes up as well.)*

ANN: Baby... Let go. Come on baby, let go.... Gimme. Gimme it baby. *(Takes the pillow)* Good... That's good. I'm gonna touch you baby.... Easy. Take it easy. *(Rubs his neck)* Good... That's good.... Let go. Come on, let it go. *(He slowly lays his head onto her lap.)* Good. That's good baby.... Good. *(Sings an Italian song to him)*
Nana nina nana oh
Questo bimbo ch'io lo do
Ch'io lo do alla bafana
Que lo tiena una set demana

(Overlap to:)

Scene Five
NOW

(Lights on CHARLIE *and* WENDY *lying in bed. The scene opens with the sound of an alarm clock.* CHARLIE *wakes up and turns it off with a sweeping motion of his hand. A baby is heard crying in the other room.* CHARLIE *tugs at* WENDY.*)*

WENDY: Whatta ya pullin' for? *(*CHARLIE *says nothing.)* Can you shut that kid up and let me sleep?

CHARLIE: He's hungry. *(The baby cries louder.)* He's hungry!

WENDY: Jesus, whatta you gotta yell for? Ah. Ah! You goin' deaf or somethin'?

CHARLIE: I said he's hungry!

WENDY: Alright.

CHARLIE: *(Whisper)* Wendy, I got a hard on.

WENDY: So jerk off.

CHARLIE: I'm hard as a rock.

WENDY: What are you crazy, Charlie? It's mornin', you filthy pig.

CHARLIE: You don't call me pig when I'm on top of you.

WENDY: How can I when you're slobbering all over my face.

CHARLIE: Well then go take care of your kid. Then go see the kid. He's hungry!

(WENDY gets up and opens the fridge door.)

WENDY: Where's the formula?

CHARLIE: I drank it.

WENDY: Charlie, how many times...

CHARLIE: Well you don't buy no soda no more.

(As WENDY pours some milk into a dirty bottle:)

CHARLIE: Don't give that kid milk. He chokes on it. Want him to die or something?

WENDY: Yeah, I want him to die.

CHARLIE: Yeah, I think you do.

(WENDY puts a piece of bread in the toaster.)

CHARLIE: Make me some toast.

WENDY: Make your own toast.

CHARLIE: You put one slice in?

WENDY: Yeah. And it's for me.

CHARLIE: Nice.

(WENDY goes into the baby's room.)

WENDY *(Off)* Here you go sweetheart. Don't choke on the cold milk your no-good father left you.

(CHARLIE turns on the clock radio.)

WENDY: Can't you wait 'til I leave?

CHARLIE: I wanna get the scores from the west coast.

WENDY: *(Comes back in)* Charlie, you were gonna get the formula.

CHARLIE: You're his mother.

WENDY: The formula is for the kid, I don't know what you're drinking it for.

CHARLIE: I DON'T KNOW WHAT TO GET 'IM, HE'S YOUR GOD-DAMN ROTTEN KID.

WENDY: Just don't drink his formula.

(She goes into the bathroom.)

CHARLIE: With a mother like you this kid don't need the boogie man.

WENDY: Fuck you.

(The phone rings. CHARLIE ignores it. It keeps ringing.)

CHARLIE: The phone is ringing. Hey Wendy, the phone is ringing. THE PHONE IS RINGING.

(She opens the bathroom door, partially dressed. The phone stops before she gets to it.)

CHARLIE: It stopped.

WENDY: You saw it ringin'.

CHARLIE: It's not for me.

WENDY: What the hell's your problem? You trying to spite me or somethin'?

CHARLIE: It's your god-damn phone, so you answer it.

WENDY: Shut up. *(Opens the window)* Ma! MA! DID YOU CALL ME? YEAH, COME ON OVER. *(Looking up)* WHAT, SO DON'T LISTEN! NOBODY UP HERE WOKE YOU UP. WE AIN'T SCREAMIN'! CAN'T SOMEBODY TALK TO THEIR OWN MOTHER IN

THIS BUILDING? MA, STAY OUT OF IT. MA,
LEMME HANDLE IT.

CHARLIE: Do I gotta get outta bed?

WENDY: WHAT YOU SAY ABOUT MY MOTHER?
LOOK, IF YOU BOTHA ME AND MY FAMILY
AGAIN I'M GONNA MAKE YOUR FACE LOOK
WORSE THEN IT LOOKS NOW.... NO, FUCK YOU
AND *YOUR* MOTHER. YEAH, YEAH, COME ON
OVER, MA. *(To* CHARLIE*)* My ma's comin' over.

CHARLIE: Tell her to bring over some donuts.

WENDY: You know where the window is, tell her
yourself.

CHARLIE: I'm starving.

WENDY: I'm tired of having some dumb ass-guinea lay
around all the time.

CHARLIE: What you gonna do about it?

WENDY: I'm gonna break your fuckin' legs!

(The baby starts crying.)

CHARLIE: Nice. You use that fuckin' language around
the kid he's gonna be a two-bit whore just like you.

WENDY: What time is it?

CHARLIE: Give me the remote. Give me the remote.

WENDY: *(Gives him remote as she tries to get ready)*
What time is it?

CHARLIE: What am I, a clock? *(Smoke comes out of the
toaster)* Hey wife, your toast is burning.

WENDY: *(Runs to toaster)* You saw it burning, you jerk.

CHARLIE: It ain't my breakfast.

WENDY: The toaster's broken. Can you fix it?

CHARLIE: I lost my tools.

WENDY: Fuck. It's 7:40. I gotta eat out.

CHARLIE: Wastin' my money all over the place.

WENDY: Your money? I'm the only one workin' here!

(She starts spraying her hair.)

CHARLIE: Go ahead. Rub it in.

WENDY: What that you don't have a job?

CHARLIE: I'm waitin' for my union card. *(The baby begins to cry.)* Go see what the kid wants.

WENDY: *(Puts on coat and starts rummaging through her purse)* I'm busy.

CHARLIE: I DON'T CARE, HE'S YOUR FUCKIN' KID SO GO TAKE CARE OF HIM.

WENDY: FOR CHRIS' SAKE, CAN'T YOU SHUT UP FOR TWO MINUTES? *(A pounding is heard from upstairs. WENDY and CHARLIE start screaming at the noise.)* Oh my God.

CHARLIE: SHUT THE FUCK UP!

WENDY: CAN'T A WOMAN TALK TO HER HUSBAND? HUH?!

CHARLIE: MIND YOUR GODDAMN BUSINESS!!

WENDY: I'M GONNA COME UP AND GET YOU!!! *(Door buzzer rings)* Where are my keys?

(A knock is heard as she starts looking around)

CHARLIE: Somebody's knockin' at the door.

WENDY: It's my mother.

CHARLIE: I can't hear you, somebody's knockin'.

WENDY: Can't you even answer the door?

CHARLIE: Wendy will be there in a minute.

WENDY: *Where are my keys?*

CHARLIE: These keys?

(He tosses her a set of keys as he presses the remote. We hear blasting TV noise.)

WENDY: Why don't you get a job.

CHARLIE: What? I can't hear you. I'm watchin' TV.

WENDY: AND WASH YOUR UNIFORM, IT STINKS.

(She goes to the door as the baby starts crying loudly.)

CHARLIE: I'm takin' it to my mother's. Your mother don't do shit.

WENDY: AND GET SOME FORMULA.

(She exits.)

CHARLIE: GIVE ME SOME MONEY! Some fuckin' mother.

(Overlap to:)

Wendy #1

WENDY: First time Charlie and me got together was like a year ago. Charlie, he always had a crush on me, I could tell. I'd catch him so scared and embarrassed of me, but always actin' like a tough guy. I'd asked him to go get me a Carvel vanilla ice cream cone with chocolate sprinkles and he was gone and back in seconds. And if he was good, I'd let him watch me eat it.

(Overlap to:)

Scene Six
THEN

(Lights up on the boys. This time the game they are playing is one in which one of the boys is between the other two. The surrounding boys are punching him in the back and kidneys when he is turned. The game consists of them punching the center man until he can block a punch. The person he blocks takes his position. The scene opens with the boys playing this game for a short while. ROCKY is in the middle.)

ED: I don't think he's even playin'.*(Punch)*

CHARLIE: You're the monkey in the middle. *(Punch)*

ED: You don't like playin' with us no more? *(Punch)*

CHARLIE: Gotta have three to play monkey in the middle.

ROCKY: There's cops all over.

ED: Cops don't give two shits when a nigger gets hit. They're gonna forget this like it was a parking ticket.

CHARLIE: Drop it. You didn't do nothin' to stop it in the first place.

ROCKY: What's the point in feedin' them balloon babies in Africa?

ED: *(Laughing)* People feed them, but that don't mean they wanna live with 'em. *(Punch)* Like at the zoo.

CHARLIE: You can't even take the subway no more. *(Punch)*

ED: Hey, Disney's on TV.... It ain't a small world. It's big and cold. Like ice. *(Punch)*

CHARLIE: I can't walk a block through Red Hook without a knife in my belly. Rocky, you gonna play!? *(Punch)*

ROCKY: *(Blocks his punch)* You're the monkey in the middle!

*(*CHARLIE *finally ends up in the center.)*

ROCKY: Fuck this, let's grab a beer. *(Punch)*

ED: I'm tired of that piss. *(Punch)*

ROCKY: Anything on? *(Punch)*

ED: I can get in for Arsenio. *(Punch)*

ROCKY: Fuck Arsenio. I got too much on my mind. Let's get laid. *(Punch)*

ED: I ain't into fuckin' them old rubber dolls at the Wrong Number. *(Punch)*

ROCKY: Michelle my belle ain't old. Second date she let me in. All I had to hand her was the love bullshit. I love you Michelle. *(Punch)*

ED: Think you can fix me up with her? *(Punch)*

ROCKY: Don't know, the bitch is picky. *(Punch)*

ED: I don't get it, a wimp like you getting laid every night. *(Punch)*

ROCKY: You gotta know how to talk to women. Look Ed, you can't just grab your prick and grunt "Fuck" and expect to get laid. You gotta have class, get dressed up and look sharp. You gotta know how to talk to a girl so she creams.

ED: How about you Charlie?

ROCKY: Get any pussy lately?

CHARLIE: Yeah.

ED: Hey, Charlie got laid. *(Punch)*

ROCKY: So that's where you been: gettin' fucked all week.

ED: I figured you got a VCR.

ROCKY: Shit Charlie, you shoulda told us. We woulda had a goodbye party for ya.

ED: I thought somethin' smell around here. *(Punch)*

CHARLIE: Time out. I gotta talk...it's important.

ROCKY: Time out Ed. *(He punches hard.)*

ED: Time out. *(Punches even harder, bending CHARLIE over)* So talk.

CHARLIE: You know Wendy?

ROCKY: The Sicilian whore. Join the club. She falls in love with somebody every ten minutes. Everybody's done her. She drives that fuckin' psycho Richie crazy.

ED: He's gonna kill ya.

CHARLIE: Yeah, I know. I got her in the basement of the projects.

ED: You smell like it.

CHARLIE: I been sleepin' there.

ROCKY: What the hell you talkin' about?

CHARLIE: I ain't taken a shower in a week.

ED: Wha' happen?

CHARLIE: You wanna hear?

ED: That's why we're listenin'.

ROCKY: Go ahead, go.

CHARLIE: I was flyin'. I musta had four or five ludes in me. Shit she looked good. Big tits wavin' out to here. They looked like Goodyear blimps under the spotlight.

ROCKY: She looks great without a shirt, don't she?

CHARLIE: Yeah, yeah, I scored big that night. You know Joanie, who works at the drugstore. She fuckin' creams every time she sees me. So she gives me about ten ludes.

ED: Is this about Joanie Big Ass or Wendy Big Tits?

CHARLIE: So Wendy starts tellin' me about how this guy she loved dumped her in the park or somethin'. I don't know. I see her and I'm really horny—fuck, I had her fucked in every possible position before we was even talking.

ROCKY: So come on, when'd ya do her?

CHARLIE: Yeah...so she's hurtin'. She's coked and I smell all this cheap liquor that's like poured all over her. And all of a sudden I see her lookin' at my cock that's bulgin' out of my pants. So I look at her and stick my hand on her tit. She pulls herself close and starts rubbin' her ass on my balls. So I give her a pair of ludes and she starts shakin' all over the place.

ED: What you do?

CHARLIE: I'm a little scared now, see, 'cause I figure maybe I'm losin' her on the coke.

ROCKY: Nah, that's how she gets when she's excited.

CHARLIE: You're right 'cause all of a sudden she falls on me and grabs my balls. So I fall down and she falls down. Face first right on my balls. I thought I was gonna come right there. So I pick her up and carry her over to the projects. On the way, I get me a fifth of Jack. On the way I put my hand down her pants and stick a finger in her—

ED: Will you stop bull-shittin'....

CHARLIE: You wanna hear the details or what?

ED: Sure just speed it up.

CHARLIE: So we get down there and the place smells like piss, lots of it. My stomach turns. And I throw up. You shoulda seen the roaches runnin' around in that green shit.

ED: You see, this is the kinda detail I don't need. I don't fuckin' need this Charlie!

CHARLIE: What?

ROCKY: Will you get to it.

CHARLIE: So I put her down on this stack of papers. I give her some ludes and a shot of Jack to wash it down. But she turns all red and is shakin' real bad. I was sure I fuckin' killed her.

ROCKY: So what you do?

CHARLIE: I jump on her and grab her arms. And try to stop this shakin' that's drivin' me fuckin' nuts!

ROCKY: How'd you stop it?

CHARLIE: We start kissin'. French kisses, disgusting, sticky, her clammy tongue way down my mouth. It tasted like the fuckin' East River.

ED: Once again, whatta ya tryin' to do, gross me out or somethin'?

ROCKY: Yeah Charlie, you're makin' me sick.

CHARLIE: And she's cryin'.

ED: So you do her?

CHARLIE: She just don't stop cryin'.

ED: Did you do her?!

CHARLIE: So I pulled down her underwears. And she pissed in them. She pissed in her fuckin' underwears.

ED: That's it, I'm gonna hit you.

(ROCKY *holds* ED *back.*)

CHARLIE: *(Starting to cry)* My folks kicked me out of the house....

ROCKY: She dead?

CHARLIE: Worse, she's pregnant.

ROCKY: Hey, wait a second. You did her a week ago, and she's pregnant? Bullshit! She's pullin' your chain.

CHARLIE: No man, I held the cup and she peed in it. I saw it change colors.

ED: You did her a week ago? When?

CHARLIE: No, I didn't say a week ago.

ED: Then when?

CHARLIE: *(Pause)* Two months ago.

ED: I'm hurt. Why didn't you tell me?

CHARLIE: I like her.

ED: At least take a shower at the gym. You smell like some wino....

CHARLIE: What gym? I'm off the fuckin' team.

ED: Congratulations to the groom.

CHARLIE: I don't wanna get married. I don't wanna get a job. I just wanna be a kid.

ROCKY: Come on Charlie, stop cryin', it ain't cool.

CHARLIE: My life is over.

ED: *(Putting his arm around* CHARLIE*)* Pregnant on the
first try. At least you know you're good at it.... Time in.

(He punches CHARLIE *real hard.* CHARLIE *falls down,
grabbing his kidneys. He rocks on the floor like a baby.)*

CHARLIE: You fuckin' idiot, you busted my kidney.

ED: Them's the rules of the game, Dad.

(Overlap to:)

Wendy #2

WENDY: Hey, I was somethin' back then. Those guys
wanted me so bad they made up stories about me.
Look, I only slept with four guys, Rocky, a pre-med
college kid who promised me penthouses, Richie,
and yeah, Charlie....

Like an idiot I fell for Richie. God, I even wanted to tie
the knot and buy the house in Jersey. Richie was real
jealous, crazy too. They used to say he took medicine to
calm him down. Once Dennis, some kid, jokin' grabbed
my tit so Richie closed a car door on his head. I think it
was a Buick, fuckin' heavy doors on Buicks. Richie, he
treated me like a princess. A fur coat. I don't think it
was legal....

But Charlie, fuckin' Charlie. The big dummy goes and
sells his comic book collection to buy me a brand-new
French-made 10-speed bike. It was sweet, I was scared.
I gave the bike to Richie as a gift so Charlie wouldn't
get his head smashed in....

That Saturday night somebody told Richie I fucked
Charlie for the bike. Fuckin' liars, pigs and liars all over
this place! At seven o'clock Mass that night, with my
folks in church, Richie throws the bike off the roof. I see

it fly past the stained glass windows, and it hits the floor, bendin' and bouncin' all ways. All the old Italian penguins dressed in black rubbin' their rosary beads come outta the church cursin' and swearin' in Latin....

He beat the shit out of me. He did disgusting things to me that night. How can I forget. I was bleeding. I wanted to die but I couldn't. Charlie, he was just there....

But he couldn't kill me either. Fifteen & pregnant. I don't even know what it's like to be a kid.

(Overlap to:)

Scene Seven
THEN

(Lights return on WENDY. CHARLIE *tosses a baseball.)*

CHARLIE: I got it.

WENDY: It's dark already.

CHARLIE: 'Cause it's night.

WENDY: So whatta ya keep bouncin' for?

CHARLIE: I'm joinin' Gil Hodges.

WENDY: What, pee wee league?

CHARLIE: Ty Cobb.

WENDY: You're eighteen.

CHARLIE: I got a fake I.D.

WENDY: You're the only guy I know who would fake his I.D. to get younger.

CHARLIE: It's my I.D., I can do whatever I want with it.

WENDY: You gettin' a job?

CHARLIE: We ain't married yet.

WENDY: I don't give a fuck if you don't marry me. I don't give a fuck if nobody marries me.

CHARLIE: I said I would, didn't I?

WENDY: But I don't give a fuck. You understand.

CHARLIE: I understand you don't give a fuck.

WENDY: What colors for the wedding?

CHARLIE: We gotta pick a color too?

WENDY: My mother won't let me wear white.

CHARLIE: I don't care. Brown, like shit.

WENDY: Fuck you.

CHARLIE: BLUE! Like the Mets.

WENDY: Orange. Orange and black.

CHARLIE: Like the Orioles.

WENDY: Like Halloween.

CHARLIE: Yeah. That's good.

(WENDY *looks up to the sky. She shakes her head.*)

WENDY: Hey, where's the Big Dipper?

CHARLIE: In my pants.

WENDY: In your dreams.

CHARLIE: Did you fuck a lot a guys?

WENDY: Some people see animals and stuff up there.

CHARLIE: You gonna keep fuckin' a lota guys?

WENDY: I don't see nothin'.

CHARLIE: WENDY!

WENDY: NO!

CHARLIE: Me neither...

WENDY: Like you did.

CHARLIE: ...All I see is a bunch a stars.

WENDY: That's somethin'.

CHARLIE: How come nobody told me howda be an astronaut?

WENDY: Like on TV?

CHARLIE: Nobody told me. Even if I ain't into it. NOBODY SAID, CHARLIE, THIS IS HOW YOU BECOME AN ASTRONAUT.

WENDY: I'll tell you. You get in your rocket ship and blast off.

CHARLIE: *(Smacks her off her head)* SHUT UP!

WENDY: *(Kicks him)* DON'T HIT ME.

CHARLIE: Oh, sorry.

WENDY: Don't fuckin' not hit me 'cause I'm pregnant. Don't hit me 'cause I'll break your ass.

CHARLIE: Don't make fun of me.

WENDY: I didn't.

CHARLIE: We're gettin' married, you know.

WENDY: I told you I don't give a fuck if you don't marry me.

CHARLIE: Alright, already.

WENDY: Lemme ask you somethin'. Did I enjoy it?

CHARLIE: You don't know?

WENDY: No, I do.... But did I enjoy it?

CHARLIE: You were red and shakin' and screamin'.... Yeah. You enjoyed it.

WENDY: Good.

(Overlap to:)

Wendy #3

WENDY: I'll tell you somethin'. I got a kid now. And sometimes in the mornin' it's a three-ring circus. And fuckin' Charlie, he wants a dog and a cat, a fish and a bird. Guy wants to live in the zoo. We got a kid, who the hell needs pets? Some nights, when Charlie ain't around, I go into his room. And I look at him, and he's

so quiet, I just start to laugh. Really, I laugh out loud.
My kid is gonna have more, I tell ya....

(Overlap to:)

Scene Eight
NOW

(Lights up on ED *and* ANN *in bed.* ED *is up and is laying on
his back, staring at the ceiling.* ANN *is curled up and laying
on her side. She tosses a few times and eventually sits up.*
ED *never looks at her.)*

ANN: Do you hear her? She's probably still sleepin'.
*(*ED *says nothing.)* She's gonna have to go to the john
soon. *(He is still.)* You goin' to work today, or maybe
you can stay home?

ED: Maybe, maybe not.

ANN: All the time maybe, maybe you could stay home
and get a wink.

ED: I would just fill in the backyard. I already pulled it
up. I gotta mix the concrete.

ANN: It'll be nice for her. She can roll herself around
back there. But if my father knew...he planted all that.

ED: We'll paint it green, like it was grass.

ANN: The light's hittin' your eyes? I'll close the shades.

ED: I gotta go to work. He's always fuckin' with me.

ANN: You know what I say about that.

ED: He acts like teachin' me how to cut the leg of a chair
is some big favor. It don't make me a slave.

ANN: You can't say fuck like that when we got a kid.

ED: This pillow is hot.

ANN: Shhh! Let's try it before she wakes up. We'll be
quiet, alright?

ED: There's too many feathers in this pillow. It's too hot.

ANN: And the doctor says it's a good time. He don't know how much time my mother takes—turn the pillow over, it's cooler on the other side.

ED: We gotta get pillows with less feathers.

ANN: It's the sheets you're fightin'.

ED: I'm sweatin' so bad the sheets feel like I'm swimmin' in 'em. We don't need all the covers.

ANN: I like the weight. It makes me feel safe.

ED: *(Gets up)* I could drop the dresser on you.

ANN: I could rub your stomach, like you were an alligator. We could get under the covers and try last night over.

ED: Your mother's up. I don't know what she needs that alarm for. Where's she goin' anyway?

ANN: *(As* ED *swallows four aspirin)* You shouldn't take four at a time.

ED: It's just aspirin. Two don't do shit.

ANN: Yeah and you eat 'em like candy. Look at me. When we first got together you'd always be touchin' my face. Lookin' at my face.

ED: There, I looked at you.

ANN: You were like sharpenin' your teeth bad last night.

ED: Was it loud?

ANN: The doctor gave you that thing.

ED: It's a bit. That's what they put in a horse.

ANN: I think horses sleep standing up, just like you.

ED: Jesus Christ. Look, I'm havin' nightmares that's all.... I don't mind waking up in a sweat, it's refreshing.

ANN: The same one?

ED: Like a horror movie.

ANN: With or without the bat?

ED: It's a dream alright, it don't mean anything.

ANN: It was loud.

ED: Did I say anythin'?

ANN: No, your teeth... Maybe, we should go see somebody about it.

ED: I don't gotta see nobody about a dream.

ANN: We'll talk to the priest.

ED: No. I ain't been to church since I was five. God don't give a shit what happens to me.

ANN: Do it for me.

ED: Alright, I'll go. Now go do somethin' for me. Make me breakfast. Forget about me, your mother's probably starvin' by now.

ANN: You're under too much pressure.

ED: I don't need no psycho-artist.

ANN: Yeah, but...

ED: Don't gimme any of that afternoon television bullshit.

ANN: Always workin' late. Maybe it's work.

ED: Maybe he don't stop fuckin' with me.... The other day, he gets me to grab the coffees. If I go for some coffee, I'll ask. But I don't need nobody, nobody tellin' me to get coffee.

ANN: My uncle got you the job.

ED: And I do my job.

ANN: He owns the place.

ED: He turns to me...and starts tellin' me to stop askin' the colored guys to get coffee. Then in front of all 'em and the spics, too, he tells me to get them coffee. I was ready to knock a tooth outta his skull.

ANN: Did you get it?

ED: It ain't like jobs grow on trees.

ANN: You only been there a year.

ED: I shoulda peed in his coffee. (ANN *silently laughs.*)
Are you laughin' at me?

ANN: No. I'm smilin'.

ED: Why?

ANN: Because we're talkin' here. It's too much caffeine.
Ya see, that's the problem.

ED: If I don't drink it, I can't stay on my feet.

ANN: Put your head in my lap.

ED: (*Gets back on bed and lays his head in her lap*) It's too
bad your mother's up.

ANN: You go from hot to cold. Who are you Ed?

ED: I'm the coffee man. You want coffee?

ANN: (*Whispers in his ear and kisses it*) You know that.

ED: Me too.

ANN: (*Kisses him and pulls back*) What was that?
You almost bit my tongue off.

ED: ...a kiss...

ANN: I'm worried.

ED: You don't got somethin' you want? I get you and
your mother everything you's want. We got a beautiful
sofa, a brand-new color television. A car. Whatta you
got to worry about? Nothin'. But you're always fuckin'
with me.

ANN: Stop sayin' that. It's always "fuckin'". I hate that
expression.

ED: So stop fuckin' with me.

ANN: I worry when you come home late and take
your dick out and try to kill me with it. It's like you're
workin' a damn jack hammer. I didn't know what you
were lookin' at.

ED: You want a kid don't you?

ANN: You didn't even come.

ED: But you did.

ANN: Did I do somethin'?

ED: *(Touches her face)* Sometimes you're so small. You seem like a kid.

ANN: This is important to me.

ED: *(Caresses her face)* I know.

ANN: I love you.

ED: *(Grabs her face)* I love you too.

ANN: You're squeezing me.

ED: It'll be alright.

ANN: You're squeezing too hard.

ED: It'll be okay.

ANN: LET GO!

(Overlap to:)

Scene Nine
NOW

(Coney Island. ROCKY and LINDA are in bed, making love. She jumps up and out.)

LINDA: No, no, no, no. I can't get the desk clerk outta my head.

ROCKY: Why do you keep gettin' outta bed like that, you're gonna hurt me.

LINDA: Did you see the look he gave me?

ROCKY: That's the way he looks.

LINDA: You come here a lot?

ROCKY: What's a lot?

LINDA: A lot.

ROCKY: I like to get out of the neighborhood.

LINDA: He looked at me like I was a hooker. We been checkin' in here for months and he looks at me like that. You come here a lot?

ROCKY: We're in the room, right, so why don't we use it.

LINDA: Some room, where's the view? This window's the size of a peephole.

ROCKY: We got a beautiful view of the ceiling.

LINDA: I wanna see the water.

ROCKY: Why?

LINDA: Because it's funny

ROCKY: I never thought about it, but yeah, water is funny.

LINDA: Not, funny funny. You never think of Brooklyn as havin' water. Like a beach. If I squint my eyes, it looks like some island you see in a magazine or a—

ROCKY: Like a waitin' room—at a doctor's office— that's where I read a magazine at.

LINDA: You sick or somethin'?

ROCKY: Nah, it's, they got sofas. You sit there, nobody bothers you. Air conditioners. Heat. Sometimes coffee.

LINDA: I know what you're waitin' for in them waitin' rooms. Some old lady with an ache. Whatta you a doctor now?

ROCKY: You sure talk a lot for a motel room. We're payin' by the hour.

LINDA: I got money. Just 'cause I need a position.

ROCKY: Position. Why don't you get a job?

LINDA: I been in hotel rooms where they put a little piece of chocolate on your pillow. And a lady comes in and pulls your sheets down for you.

ROCKY: Linda, this is Brooklyn, we can make our own beds.

LINDA: I wish it was rainin', that's romantic.

ROCKY: I could turn on the shower.

LINDA: You said—

ROCKY: Yeah, I like the smell of this room. It smells like funk.

LINDA: You don't gotta prove anything. Just 'cause you're white and shit. Italians are half black anyways.

ROCKY: I know.

LINDA: Whatta you tell your friends? I sing the blues, what?

ROCKY: What you tell yours, I'm the Italian Stallion, who smells like a scallion?

LINDA: That's the stupidest thing I ever heard.

ROCKY: This is a lotta talking for a motel room. They got benches for that.

LINDA: We been on benches, we don't talk.

ROCKY: That's why we got a great relationship.

LINDA: Tell me about your family.

ROCKY: They don't talk much.

LINDA: You want it or not?

ROCKY: I come from a family of tailors. My father always looked good. I was wearin' suits to kindergarten. He made a suit for Walt Frazier once. I know how to cut a pattern. I could cut you outta paper.

LINDA: Like them paper dolls, you make as kids, never like those, all lined up like that.

ROCKY: Now, when I see my father, it's like we both forgot somethin'.

LINDA: My father would tell me to make believe the storm was like a band playin' or somethin'. Now, I make believe the train is like a storm. Like the sparks are like lightnin' and the thunder.

ROCKY: I could spit out your window and hit somebody on the B-train.

LINDA: Sometimes after you go, I keep shakin'.

ROCKY: That's how it is when we have sex. It's like pizza. Even when it's okay, it's pretty good.

LINDA: Fuck, I gotta go.

ROCKY: I thought you liked this room. It's Coney Island. It's not a part of Brooklyn. It's quiet. 'Cept for the waves, they make a lotta noise.

LINDA: My kids are down the hall. And they don't go to school till I kiss 'em good mornin'.

ROCKY: Why ain't they sleepin' at your place?

LINDA: The faucet is busted. Hot water don't stop comin' out. You walk in, there's like a fog. Like it's sunny outside but it's gonna rain in my house, I'm scared one of 'em is gonna go for a drink or to wash a hand and get really burned.

ROCKY: I gotta put a wrench to it.

LINDA: I need a plumber.

ROCKY: Baby, I know plumbing. Doctor, plumber, what's the difference?

LINDA: How about a cop? You and two black kids down that avenue.

ROCKY: It's a feast. We'll get a couple of sausage and peppers. Take a ride. Win a doll. The Feast of St. Jude, saint of lost causes.

LINDA: No, this is not funny. You're talkin' about my love.

ROCKY: "Come back on the raft, you're drownin' out there!"

LINDA: I could come over to your place later.

ROCKY: I don't have a bed.

LINDA: You know there's a time difference, when you walk into Bensonhurst? It's like forty years ago.

ROCKY: I really don't have a bed. I never needed one before. I don't even know how to sleep alone.

LINDA: This is not about your bed. When we took the B train over here, I looked down at your neighborhood and it looks like little matchboxes. Tiny little matchboxes.

ROCKY: I love you.

LINDA: What?

ROCKY: Holy shit.

LINDA: Did you just say somethin'?

ROCKY: Yeah, fuck, I said I love you.

LINDA: Oh, no, this can't be happenin'.

ROCKY: I'm sorry.

LINDA: We got problem.

ROCKY: I can fix it.

LINDA: You asshole.

ROCKY: *(Pause. He goes over and gives her a kiss.)* Close your eyes.

LINDA: I don't like doin' that.

ROCKY: I closed my eyes, why don't you close yours?

LINDA: If your eyes are closed how come you know mine ain't?

ROCKY: If your eyes are open, then you'd know that mine are closed.

LINDA: Rocky, what did you tell the desk clerk?

ROCKY: Come on.

LINDA: No, really.

ROCKY: *(Pause)* I told him that you were my wife.

LINDA: Oh, no. I just got one of those chills that comes from nowhere.

ROCKY: You like the rain?

LINDA: *(Nods her head)* Yeah.

ROCKY: *(Starts to kiss her)* Good, 'cause I'm like the rain 'cause I fall like little kisses all over you, and I'm like the wind because I pick you up and take you, and I'm like the lightning

LINDA: So you're a storm.

ROCKY: Yeah.

(They kiss.)

Ann #1

ANN: "This country it kill you for a dollar," that's what my father always said. And it did. My father was made of twigs near the end. Like he didn't have bones, but branches.... For as long as I can remember, I kept thinkin' he's gonna break....

He barely spoke English. He couldn't even fill out a "what's your name" form. I was on my way to college but we ran out of money, my father's money. The medical bills and the medicine was too much. We knew he was going to die....

This hurts, but sometimes I wonder if it was worth keeping him alive....

I used to walk home from school, slow. I didn't know what was waitin' for me when I got home. I was payin' bills, and writin' checks when I was twelve. My parents, their English is not too good. The first time I saw Ed was more than, no, a couple of years ago. It was one of those afternoons, late, that time a day when the colors change. I can remember exactly how he moved. I can't even remember what I ate, but I remember exactly how he moved. It was like the muscles in his arms were floating, like he had clouds in there. I just wanted him to pick me up, I wanted to sit in his arms like he was a tree.... *(Overlap to:)*

Scene Ten
THEN

(Lights up on the boys. This time, the action of the scene is that each boy is trying to stick a finger up the other boy's buttocks or slap him with a limp backhand to the groin. If they succeed in the groin, they say "duck". In the buttocks, they say "goose". It is a game they often play. CHARLIE has a bag with an open wine bottle in it that they pass around.)

ED: Don't be drinking that poison.

CHARLIE: What?

ED: Wine ain't supposed to fizz.

CHARLIE: It's apple wine. Doctor's away and shit.

ED: It'll burn little holes in your stomach. They put in antifreeze. *(ED ducks CHARLIE.)*

CHARLIE: Where the fuck is wine gonna freeze?

ED: Stick it in the freezer. It don't freeze. My uncle puts it in his radiator.

(He gooses CHARLIE.)

ROCKY: Science, I tell ya.

CHARLIE: Maybe that's why I throw up every morning.

ROCKY: Hey Ed, sweetie. Heard you took a honeymoon with a faggot-ass.

(He gooses ED.)

ED: Bullshit.

ROCKY: That's the word.

ED: Who said it? Who? I'll break his fuckin' legs!

(ED ducks ROCKY.)

ROCKY: Word is they did you in the bar under the bridge.... Ain't that the word, Charlie?

(He gooses CHARLIE.)

CHARLIE: Fuck up man.

(He ducks ROCKY, *who then gooses him. They start bouncing around and trying to smack each other.)*

ED: Boys. Boys. *(They don't stop.)* Cut the shit!
(They stop.) It was nothin'.

CHARLIE: We were flyin'. We were celebratin', the guy died a retard. He never fingered us....

ED: So now you can shut up about it already.

CHARLIE: Ed, didn't them fuckin' girls look beautiful?
Didn't they?

ED: I coulda sworn they was girls.

CHARLIE: You shoulda seen them swayin' and bumpin' their round asses all over the dance floor.

ED: It was blonde night. You get free drinks if you was blonde. Blondes all over. I love blondes.

CHARLIE: And what a blonde. She had tits out to here.
I mean he had tits. Shit, I mean he looked like he had tits. It had tits out to here. I'm confused.

ED: She was gorgeous.

(He ducks ROCKY.*)*

CHARLIE: Even if she was a guy, I swear.

*(*ED *ducks him. He doubles over.)*

ED: She was definitely the best looking out there.

ROCKY: She was a he?

CHARLIE: She was real sexy. She goes to Ed, "Why don't you come out with me?"

ED: I figured I'm gonna score with a woman. Not some girl.

CHARLIE: She was all over him. They were makin' out on the dance floor like newlyweds. Show him the hickey, Ed.

ED: Shut up Charlie. Shut the fuck up. You know, you don't know when to keep that dumb-ass mouth shut. One day I'm gonna knock it off your face. Now shut up. That stuff ain't important.

ROCKY: So when you fuck the faggot ass?

ED: I didn't.... I just go out when she—he—grabs me in the alley. And starts playing the skin flute. I didn't know what's happenin'.

CHARLIE: Then's when I came out and I saw her goin' on him like a locomotive. Chug a chug. She was flyin' up and down, up and down.

ED: Shut up. Who's tellin' this story, you or me?

CHARLIE: You.

ED: So why you gotta open your mouth all the time. If I'm tellin' the story, let me tell the story.

CHARLIE: Alright, tell the story. Just you ain't tellin' it right.

ED: Look, if I want you to tell it, I'll tell ya.

ROCKY: So when you fuck him?

ED: I didn't fuck no faggot.... Now I see her flyin' on me up and down. I mean, no girl's gonna do what she likes. Like the man is gotta be in control. Right?

ROCKY: Right.

ED: Right Charlie?

CHARLIE: Oh, so I can talk now?

ED: Yeah.

CHARLIE: Right Ed.

ED: So I decide to give her what she wants. I'm gonna fuck her brains out. So I reach for her snatch....

CHARLIE: That's when this big tremendous dick flies out. And guess what, it wasn't Ed's.

ED: Charlie you're pissin' me off. (*He ducks* CHARLIE *hard.*) Shut up.

ROCKY: Sounds like the story goin' 'round. Ed the fag-fucker.

ED: Shut your mouth... So, I see this big tremendous dick fly out, and it wasn't mine. I was pissed off, so I called Charlie over and we kicked the shit out of him....

CHARLIE: I held him down and Ed jammed a bottle up his ass. (ED *stares at* CHARLIE *and then ducks him*) I'm just finishing the story.

ED: Charlie held him down. But I was just teachin' a lesson that's all. Fuckin' no-good dirty AIDS-ass faggot.

CHARLIE: Ed was like an animal.

ED: (*Smacks* CHARLIE) Shut up! I was just teachin' him a lesson.

ROCKY: Well Ed, the whole school's thinkin' maybe you like to give it up the ass.... Maybe you is the fag.

ED: Who said that? I'll kill them.

ROCKY: But don't worry Ed, all the great artists were butt-fuckers. Hey Ed, maybe you're a great artist.

(*He gooses* ED.)

CHARLIE: Yeah, a bullshit artist.

ED: You better tell me who's spreadin' that story or I'm gonna twist your peckers off.

(CHARLIE *gooses* ED *and* ROCKY *ducks him.*)

ROCKY: What if it's true, Ed, one mornin' you'll wake up and just all of sudden wanna suck cock.

CHARLIE: You'll start wearing funny girl clothes.

(CHARLIE *gooses* ED.)

ED: I ain't laughin'.

CHARLIE: Yeah and you'll be in the Village wearing leather, playin' with little boys and walkin' poodles.... Maybe it's some disease you caught from the blonde.

(ED *puts him in a headlock.*)

ED: I'll kill you.

ROCKY: Shit, Ed, huggin' boys already? I see it comin'.

ED: Charlie, grab him or I'll kill you.

CHARLIE: We's only kiddin'.

ROCKY: Whatta you gonna do to me, butt-fuck me?

ED: Charlie, grab him *(Grabs the bottle)* Who told you?

CHARLIE: How's Rocky gonna know?

(He grabs ROCKY and covers his mouth. ROCKY mumbles.)

ROCKY: Hey let go. I'll kill you, you faggot. Let go.

ED: Shut up.

(He pulls down ROCKY's pants and is ready to jam the bottle.)

ROCKY: CHARLIE. CHARLIE'S TELLIN' EVERYBODY YOU FUCKED A FAGGOT.

CHARLIE: SHUT UP!

(ED lets go of ROCKY.)

CHARLIE: He's lyin'.

ED: I'm so fuckin' stupid. *(CHARLIE runs away.)* And don't come back.

(Overlap to:)

Scene Eleven
THEN

(ED is sitting in the corner, crying. He turns and throws the bag with the bottle, which breaks. Walking across with groceries in her hands is ANN.)

ANN: Are you crying? *(He shakes his head "no".)* Father McGrail whip you? *(He shows her the palms of his hands.)* Then what's the tears?

ED: They just come out.... I don't know from where.

ANN: Babies cry when they're tired.

ED: I'm not a baby.

ANN: Are you tired?

ED: All the time.

ANN: My father can't sleep. Makes him cry all the time. He's scared he won't wake up.

ED: He's sick?

ANN: He's just gettin' skinnier. My mother says he's gonna disappear soon.

ED: You alright?

ANN: Yeah, why?

ED: You're outta breath.

ANN: Oh, there was this dog.

ED: Chased you?

ANN: Yeah, well, once. 'Cause I froze in front of this dog. And it bit me on the ankle! I wasn't doin' a thing. And it wouldn't let go. My father hadda knock it in the head with a hammer so it would stop. And I felt bad for the dog. Like it was my fault the dog's head got busted.

ED: If a dog ever bit you I would cut its fuckin' head off.

ANN: Don't talk like that.

ED: Why? I'd bring the head back for you. That's what I would do for you.

ANN: Why?

ED: So that you don't freeze.

ANN: *(Starts cleaning the glass)* You're gonna cut yourself.

ED: Maybe my blood would stop boilin' then.

ANN: You angry at somebody?

ED: It don't make sense. It's like a noise in my head all the time. Like a TV on a dead channel.

(ANN *empties out a bag of apples, one of which she gives to*
ED. *She then starts picking up pieces of glass and putting*
them in the bag.)

ANN: Apples are good for you.

ED: Doctor's away and shit.

ANN: But cuttin' yourself...

ED: You know the stained glass. The one that broke,
St. Francis. Or was it St. Anthony? Which one is the
saint of lost causes?

ANN: St. Jude.

ED: Anyways. I put my fist through a piece of it.
And I felt better.

ANN: It's a church, Ed.

ED: It's a piece of glass.

ANN: You throw rice not bottles. Whatta you so angry
about you gotta break glass?

ED: It's hard to pick the right thing to wear in the
morning. Is that hard for you too?

ANN: It's hard for everybody, I think.

ED: No. Some people got it easy. And you wanna know
why? 'Cause life ain't fair.

ANN: Yes it is....

ED: Because, why?

ANN: Because, because, God is fair.

ED: Your father's sick, right, it sounds like he's gonna
die.

ANN: I don't like it, but there must be a reason.

ED: Sounds too easy, this reason thing.

ANN: Yeah...like that man. The black guy they
murdered. He had three little boys.... What kinda
animals would do a thing like that? I don't know

sometimes why God lets things happen. I mean, there must be a reason.

ED: What's the reason?

ANN: My father, he's from Italy, and they don't do things like that. Everybody thinks all Italians are like that. But whatta you gonna do? You are Italian, so somehow it is your fault. I mean there's gotta be somethin' you can do—

ED: You think God is gonna forgive those guys?

ANN: *(As she picks up a piece of glass)* Ow! I cut myself.

ED: Let me see. *(He takes her hand.)*

ANN: It stings.

ED: Maybe a little piece is in there. *(He sucks on the wound.)*

ANN: That tickles.

ED: You think God is gonna forgive them?

ANN: Those animals.

ED: You think?

ANN: If they make up for it.

ED: And what if they don't?

ANN: God won't forgive them.

ED: I don't know. A lotta ghosts around this neighborhood would tell you otherwise.

ANN: You believe in that?

ED: So many people die around here, you gotta. I know people, fallin' outta windows, gettin' shot, run over.... God—yeah, right...

ANN: You think my father would come back as a ghost?

ED: A good ghost. He'll come back and close your eyes for you just when you're about to go to sleep.

ANN: That's pretty.

ED: Can I, can I touch your face?

ANN: Watch the apples.

ED: Can I put my head in your lap?

ANN: My hands bleedin' a little.

ED: Lemme hold it.

ANN: I don't get you, Ed. You're scared of ghosts, but you ain't scared of dogs....

ED: I'm scared of you.

ANN: You can kiss me if you want.

(Overlap to:)

Ann #2

ANN: *(As* ED *lays still)* I tell you somethin' I'll never forget. When my father died. They were bringin' him up the steps of the church in his coffin. That coffin was the most money my father ever spent on one thing in his life. And Ed—he was one of the pallbearers—when the guy in front of him slipped on some leftover rice from a wedding or something, and he falls. And the coffin starts wobblin' this way and that. And the pallbearers, their hands are gettin' twisted, and they let go. And Ed, like some kinda Atlas, goes under and holds the coffin up. The sweat pourin' down his face. His arms shakin' from the weight. And I saw him strong. I looked at him and I didn't worry about a thing.

(Blackout)

(End Act One)

ACT TWO

NOW

Linda, Wendy, & Ann

(The three women appear)

LINDA: I could see it, from the roof of my building. All those lights back there. Sometimes a ferris wheel.

WENDY: The Feast.

ANN: The Feast of St. Jude.

WENDY: It's really like a block party. A lotta dancin'. All kinda music, mixin' it up in the background. Opera. Italian. Black. All fucked up like that.

ANN: Then there is the procession.

WENDY: Yeah, these old guys, real serious, their hands look like leather. They carry the Saint around. And the suckers they come out and like take pictures of themselves pinnin' their last twenty onto the Saint's dress. Like a twenty is gonna get them into heaven. Anyways, the food is good. And every once in a while a fight breaks out. And that's exciting.

ANN: You would always see a little commotion and the next thing you know, arms are flying.

WENDY: I remember once, this time, by the wheel with the numbers. Those fuckin' guys would drop a hundred dollars to win like a stuffed banana. And these girls walkin' around with these stuffed bananas, sick!

And the next thing you know, a black kid is running
his way through the feast, and guys chasin' him.
That's how it would happen. Like that.

ANN: It always felt cold the night after the Feast.

WENDY: Rain and shit. Like overnight it was winter.
Like the rides and booths took the weather with the
money.

ANN: The little kids would go around and turn the
garbage upside down, lookin' for nickels, dimes,
sometimes a dollar.

LINDA: And that's when the black kids got to come in.
You could make a few dollars, cleanin' up the Avenue.
Sweep. Hose it down. Make sure it's clean if you want
a good tip.

ANN: I never got the gambling. The church would turn
the rectory into a casino.

WENDY: The day after, everybody was busted.
No money. The church and the games got it all.

LINDA: And from the roof, you watched them roll the
ferris wheel away.

(Overlap to:)

Scene One

(Lights up on ED *in front of the stage, kneeling with his face
to the side of the audience. His hands are clasped in prayer as
a single light shines on his face.)*

ED: Forgive me Father for I have sinned. It's been fifteen
years since my last confession. Look, I ain't been in one
of these phone booths since my dad died on the F train.
Wuz gonna take me to the Yankee game, World Series,
ya know that?

He had a heart attack at Union Square. Pencils in his
hands. They thought he was asleep. They didn't try
to wake him 'til the train yards....

The paper said it was tragic—had my glove and
sandwiches ready. It was all set. Ain't no God I figured
if I can't even see a World Series game—waited for
hours for 'im, but Dad never showed....

I got the sweats, Father. Wake up with a nightmare.
Everybody gets 'em I guess, maybe it's the year for
'em or somethin'. But mine got whips and stuff.
Painful. I get it while I'm foolin' around too. All I
wanna do half the time is puke. I don't get it Father.
Hey, anybody call you Dad....

My wife, I can't look her in the face without a knot
in my stomach. It hurts when I see her. Sometimes,
she looks so sad....

She wants a kid. I think it's an excuse to screw. I look
at kids, they look weird to me, like they come from
another planet....

It ain't bad to get crazy, it's just the way people is....

She says you can help me. She's got a good heart. Can
you help me? Ah, what the fuck do you know? Father
McGrail used to take my hand and whip it 'til it bled.
All you priests, always whippin' me for something....

If I wuz a bigger kid, I woulda got you guys back then.
You guys ever hit me again, I'll smack that collar off
your neck so hard it'll take off your head....

Wrong, right. Wrong, right. Wrong, right...

You don't know....

Ever hear someone's skull crack? Like a walnut. Ever
watch a man, beaten, lying dead, spittin' up black blood
the color of your shirt? Ever kill a man? Ever touch
another man's dick? Ever think about it? Ever take off
your collar and try to live around here? Just live...

How many Hail Mary's, how many, ten, twenty?
How 'bout a million. You think that'll help?
(Overlap to:)

Scene Two

(LINDA is sleeping on the sofa in her business clothes. ROCKY comes in. He has sheets. He slaps a sheet out and then tosses it over LINDA's resting body.)

ROCKY: What's the door doin' on the window?

LINDA: It's seven o'clock in the morning.

ROCKY: Am I late?

LINDA: How can you be late when you're not expected?

ROCKY: You got a Coke?

LINDA: Somebody make you breakfast. You want me to scramble some eggs? A dozen. How about two dozen eggs, over easy?

ROCKY: This is my breakfast. Cleans my teeth. Good for my digestion

LINDA: You gotta eat breakfast if you wanna stay young. You look like shit.

ROCKY: Thanks for the support.

LINDA: Maybe you'd like some sausages.

ROCKY: That's the kid's door? They asleep?

LINDA: Left for school... They woke up waitin' for you.

ROCKY: That's nice.... I got us some sheets. 180 threads, all cotton...80%, anyways.

LINDA: Maybe you could wear it like a ghost.

ROCKY: Maybe you could put them on the bed
and we'll fuck them up. We'll eat somethin' later.
We'll order in. Somebody's gotta deliver around here.

LINDA: You sure you don't want breakfast?

ROCKY: Linda, I gotta tell you somethin', I really don't like breakfast.

LINDA: Maybe some sausage and peppers.

ROCKY: Hey, that's Italian.

LINDA: What, I can't make sausage and peppers?

ROCKY: Just, I didn't....

LINDA: I didn't either. I went to Top Tomatoe last night at about two in the mornin'. I got some ripe, fresh peppers, green, yellow, red, all the colors of the Italian flag. That's the best thing about this crazy neighborhood, you can get fruits and vegetables twenty-four hours a day. But they didn't have sausage. So I took my life in my hands and I walked down to that deli on 86, the all-night one, where you acted like you didn't know me.

ROCKY: You did what?!

LINDA: I got the last ones, frozen. They looked at me, like I just stole the holy grail. I hadda tell them I was Sicilian. I was scared walkin' home. Not only am I black, but I got a very important piece of Italian sausage.

ROCKY: What time was this?

LINDA: Late, very late... Do I broil it, fry it, boil it, what? It's not like I got instructions. I got no idea. Who am I gonna ask? Your mother... Smoke all over the house. The kids coughin'. I threw most of it away.

ROCKY: The secret is the onions.

LINDA: They make me cry.... I coulda went to the Feast and got some myself. Get myself a sandwich, but...

ROCKY: I'm sorry.

LINDA: I made my kids sausage and peppers. I don't even know what sausage and peppers is. Sausage stickin' to the pan, burnin', smelled awful. I still smell it on my hands.

ROCKY: I said I'm sorry.

LINDA: I hadda borrow three dollars from my own kid. They went to school with their eyes bloodshot.

ROCKY: That feast is for crooks.

LINDA: You oughtta stop drinkin' that Coke, you gettin' a twitch in your eye, like a liar.

ROCKY: Hey, do you see a ring on my finger?

LINDA: No. But we got a photo album.

ROCKY: I ain't his father, where's he?

LINDA: Then don't act like it.

ROCKY: Figures.

LINDA: Whatya sayin'? I know where he's at!

ROCKY: What the hell is that door doin' on the window?

LINDA: Some people use bars, but I like a door. It keeps the sun out, the rain, the bullets—

ROCKY: Which bullet?

LINDA: The one that hit the old lady in the ceiling. Don't them cracks look like an old lady? But I figure, you walk out that door, you can step right on the platform.

ROCKY: I'm sorry. Let's make love? Then we can fight when we wake up. We'll have more energy.

LINDA: I woke up this mornin', I was havin' such a good dream about you. I didn't want you to come over.

ROCKY: Let's go to bed, we talk better there.

LINDA: I got an interview.

ROCKY: Call in sick.

LINDA: You can't call in sick to an interview.

ROCKY: I called that number in the paper...the one you gave me. Old guys in the basement. Cuttin' suits. It smelled like farts. And get this, you gotta wear a tie. Like who's gonna see a tie in the basement.... Look at me,I can't work in a cellar. Suckin' on nine to five. And don't start that college shit, I ain't kissin' ass nowhere.

LINDA: Except some old broad's wrinkled ass, for her pocket book change.

ROCKY: Last night, I was walkin' home and a sixteen-year-old girl came up to me and asked me for my autograph. You wanna know why?

LINDA: Because you fucked her mother.

ROCKY: What is that a joke? You think I like wakin' up and havin' some old lady who smells like the first floor of Macy's gummin' on my cock. Man, those are the times when you realize that we all deserve to die.

LINDA: I go to sleep in the mornin' and I get up at night. Your life is makin' me upside down.

ROCKY: I got friends. I get jobs. I bet games. I make money. And what's the one thing you can't buy? Money.

LINDA: Gotta stay top cock, the "king of the kids." —This is not a good time to be foolin' around.

ROCKY: We don't got diseases like that in my neighborhood. That's a good neighborhood.

LINDA: What?

ROCKY: Why do I always gotta say I'm sorry?

LINDA: Why do you keep comin' back here?

ROCKY: I hadda walk up eight flights of stairs. These kids are shootin' at a bottle in the elevator. They leave the door open. And they pop it as it goes by like a moving target. Like a booth at the Feast. Maybe they hit the window.

LINDA: Why do you keep comin' back?

ROCKY: What? I'll fix the window. I'll fix the sink. I'll fix the cracks in the ceiling. I'll fix the neighbor's window. I'll fix the building. I'll be the fuckin' super.

LINDA: Why do you?

ROCKY: I'll take the kids to Coney Island. I'll take them to Disneyland. I'll take them to the fuckin' Bahamas?

LINDA: Why?

ROCKY: Sheets ain't cheap.

LINDA: Oh! Am I your charity? 'Cause I don't need to be takin' care of. I don't need you to take care of us. Even the way you fuck me lately.

(He throws the white sheet over his head.)

ROCKY: Boo!

LINDA: TAKE THAT OFF! You don't even know what you do?

(The train rumbles overhead.)

ROCKY: How can you stand that noise all day?

LINDA: You didn't come over last night, because you were too scared to take my kids to your feast.

ROCKY: I come over here, I get more tired than tired.

LINDA: Too smart. Too black. Too many kids. Too pretty. Too plain. Too many toos.

ROCKY: I ain't a handyman.

LINDA: You lookin' at yourself in the mirror again?

ROCKY: That noise!

LINDA: What noise?

ROCKY: You wanna hear some story.... I love you blah, blah, blah....

LINDA: Yeah, I wanna hear story. 'Cause you said you loved me in that bedroom, you loved me in that hotel room in Coney Island, you even loved me in the back seat of that Cadillac. Say you love me now?

ROCKY: Fuck, I come here don't I? You want me to marry ya? Is that it? I got friends, I know what it's like. A year or two we're gonna hate each other. What's up? When you get tired of the taste of my breath and the smell of my feet? When the way I toss at night bothers you, what then? Is that what you want?

LINDA: I want you to make me a sausage and peppers sandwich, you wanna show me how?

ROCKY: You wanna fuck?

LINDA: Do you wanna sandwich?

ROCKY: You wanna screw, sometimes that works better?

LINDA: You want a sandwich or not?

ROCKY: I guess you don't wanna fuck.

LINDA: I guess you don't wanna sandwich.

ROCKY: I don't love anyone or anything. It don't pay. It don't work. All I feel is when I come. One day the bomb is gonna hit and blow this planet into little pieces, and I'm gonna be layin' in bed comin' and I won't even know it happened.

LINDA: 'Cause you'll be an old beat up man jerkin' off.

(Overlap to:)

Scene Three

(Lights up on WENDY *lying on the couch of her and* CHARLIE's *place.* CHARLIE's *in the next room quietly trying to dress the baby. The sound of a TV is heard.)*

WENDY: Hey what ya doin'?

CHARLIE: *(Off)* Nothin'!

WENDY: You gotta be doin' somethin'.

CHARLIE: *(Off)* Nothin'. Just dressin'!

WENDY: You goin' out again?

CHARLIE: *(Off; pause)* Bowlin' night.

WENDY: Bowlin' night? Ya ain't bowled on a Friday night since ya was a kid.

CHARLIE: *(Off)* The bar's havin' a bowlin' night.

WENDY: Bunch a drunks bowlin'. Maybe I should come?

CHARLIE: *(Off)* No, no it's just for the guys.

WENDY: Rocky goin'?

CHARLIE: *(Off)* Nah, he don't come around much no more.

WENDY: Charlie, you're missin' the best part, they're gonna burn him now. You eva notice how crazy these Indians are in these movies? Somethin' like you guys at a bowlin' alley.

CHARLIE: *(Off)* Sounds more like a party at your mother's!

WENDY: Only half-naked shit-hole is my husband. Who jumps into the shower with a bottle of vodka and my eighteen-year-old niece.

CHARLIE: *(Off)* She's on the high-school swimming team.

WENDY: She's also head cheerleader. Don't mean you gotta cheer some head.

CHARLIE: *(Off)* She ain't blood.

WENDY: And they were almost likin' you. Is Charlie sleepin'?

CHARLIE: *(Off)* He's always sleepin'.

WENDY: It's all the noise. *(We hear a burp.)* What was that? Was that the kid?

CHARLIE: *(Off)* That was me.

WENDY: IS HE UP?

CHARLIE: *(Off)* Sleepin' like a baby.

(Another burp)

WENDY: Why don't I come in there.

CHARLIE: *(Off)* Nah, I'm coming out, just buttoning my coat.

WENDY: God, you should see his flesh melt!

(CHARLIE *walks into the living room, carefully carrying a bowling bag.*)

CHARLIE: Well, gotta go.

WENDY: You sure you wanna go bowlin'? We ain't been home alone for a month now. Stay home. We'll play gin, strip, and fuck like the old days.

CHARLIE: Don't wanna be late.

(*Wanting to leave, he turns and the bowling bag burps. They both look at the bag.*)

WENDY: Your bowling bag burped.

CHARLIE: That was me.

WENDY: What's in there?

CHARLIE: Nothin', a bowlin' ball.

WENDY: WHAT THE FUCK IS MY BABY DOIN' IN THAT BOWLING BAG.... I'LL KILL YOU.

CHARLIE: There ain't no baby in here. He's in the crib.

WENDY: Let me see.

(*She goes for the bag. He pulls away.*)

CHARLIE: No.

WENDY: GIVE ME MY BABY.

CHARLIE: Look we're just going out for a walk.

WENDY: In a bowlin' bag? IT'S FREEZING OUT THERE, HE'S GONNA FREEZE TO DEATH.

CHARLIE: He ain't cold, he's in the bowlin' bag.

WENDY: HE'LL SUFFOCATE.

CHARLIE: Nah, there's some little holes to air out my shoes.

(*He goes to open the bag. She grabs one of the handles.*)

WENDY: THE KID'S STAYIN' HOME.

CHARLIE: What you doin'?

WENDY: He ain't goin'.

(They start to tug.)

CHARLIE: Let go of the fuckin' kid. We're going to my mother. You happy now? That's all, just to my mother.

WENDY: Your mother. The one who feeds him macaroni like he's dying or somethin'.

CHARLIE: He can use it.

WENDY: The kid's stayin'. I don't want her makin' him a fat little pig.

CHARLIE: LET GO, OR I'LL CRACK YOU.

WENDY: Let go and stop it. YOU CRAZY OR SOMETHIN', YOU'RE GONNA KILL HIM.

CHARLIE: YOU LET GO.

WENDY: NO.

CHARLIE: LET GO OR I'M GONNA BREAK YOUR FACE.

(They pull with such force that they both let go. The bag falls to the ground. The baby starts to cry.)

WENDY: Oh my God.

CHARLIE: See what you done you stupid bitch. You almost broke my bowlin' bag.

(She goes for the baby. He lunges forward and grabs the bag.)

WENDY: I HATE YOU. You're trying to kill him.

CHARLIE: Calm down. I'll be right back. He's my kid too.

WENDY: GIVE ME MY BABY. I HATE YOU, I HATE YOU.

CHARLIE: Yeah, yeah. Everybody hates everybody. So don't be cryin' so much. Look, you got what you want. I married you. And you got your office girl career you made such a big stink about. So stop givin' me shit.

WENDY: Where you goin'? Is it some girl?

CHARLIE: Yeah, I got fifteen blow jobs lined up for tonight.

WENDY: Yeah, well I'm going out too.

CHARLIE: *(Puts bag down on couch as he puts on his coat)*
Go ahead, go out with one of them office boys you
always talk about.

WENDY: You liked it alright. Men still find me attractive.

CHARLIE: Yeah, you make me sick.

WENDY: Give me my baby. GIVE MY MY BABY.
(She jumps for the baby on the couch.)

CHARLIE: GET OUTTA HERE.

WENDY: Give me my baby!

CHARLIE: You're really pissin' me off.

*(He punches her. She staggers and falls as he exits with the
bag.)*

WENDY: Leave him. He's Rocky's kid. He's my kid.

(CHARLIE returns.)

CHARLIE: He's whose kid?

WENDY: Rocky's.

CHARLIE: What I can't hear you.

WENDY: Rocky.

CHARLIE: I can't hear you. Are you saying something?

WENDY: IT'S ROCKY'S KID!

CHARLIE: What?

WENDY: Rocky. I fuck him all the time. Before work.
At lunch. After work. Just you're the only jerk dumb
enough to marry me.

(She's crying. CHARLIE gives her a hug. Pause.)

CHARLIE: Finders keepers, losers weepers. *(Punches her
in the eye and she twists into the fetal position. As he leaves:)*
He's mine now.

(Overlap to:)

Scene Four

(Lights come up on ANN *. She sits at the dining room table. She says her prayer in a whisper. In front of her is a white porcelain cup. In her hands, she rubs rosary beads.)*

ANN: Padre Nostro, che sei nei cieli
Sia santificato it tuo nome
Thy kingdom come, thy will be done
In cielo cosi in terra
Dacci oggi il Nostro pane quotidiano
And forgive us our trespasses
As we forgive those who trespass against us
E non ci indurre in tentazione
Ma liberaci dal malle

Amen

(She hears the door. She drops her rosary beads into her coffee cup. She stares out the window. ED *enters, a bag of cherries in his hand.)*

ED: What're you doin',rememberin'?

ANN: I looked out the window till I was five years old.

ED: I got you some cherries, from Italy. *(He offers her the bag, which she doesn't take.)*

ANN: I wasa scared to play with the kids across the street. My English wasn't so good back then.

ED: And I didn't call.

ANN: I was gonna grow Christmas trees. Why did we fill up the backyard, why?

ED: I could bust open a hole in the concrete and plant a cherry tree.

ANN: My father woulda called.

ED: Yeah, well, your father didn't work with his hands.

ANN: Dinner's endin' up tastin' like that frozen TV crap.

ED: You ain't no great cook to begin with.

ANN: She just wants us to eat like a family. She just wants the best for us.

ED: I put the food in her mouth. That's not best enough. There are places where I'm good enough.

ANN: Maybe you ate already.

ED: I really don't give a shit about dinner.

ANN: Just try to be a little more co-operative.

ED: Big word co-operative. I try to make it. But things come up.

ANN: Why were you late?

ED: I hadda redo some chair legs.

ANN: Right.

ED: I hadda redo the legs! My hands don't stop shakin'. I got glue all over my hands. Legs are stickin' to me. I even burned my finger on the saw. Every time I cut one, it snaps. I can't even cut a goddamn leg no more. Glue all over my shoes. I walk outta there, I stick to the street.

ANN: Eat if you're gonna eat.

ED: I was workin' late. What?! You don't believe me? You know that's the problem, it's not me. It's that you don't trust nobody. You're locked up in here all day with your mother, and it's makin' you a sick bitch. You oughtta get out more.

ANN: *(Unable to control her anger)* Well, this "sick bitch" called up the store, and they told me you left with somebody.

(Pause)

ED: It was one a the stock boys, needed a lift.

ANN: I didn't know you had any stock boys that wear dresses.

ED: I just walked out with her, that's all. She's as old as your mother. It's business. She's a customer.

ANN: What's her name?

ED: What?!

ANN: What's her name???

ED: How the fuck do I know? You called the store? Who did you speak to?

ANN: The kid who answered the phone.

ED: The spic. You're listening to a fuckin' spic.

ANN: You're late all week. Where do you go?

ED: I'm tired, I drive around, that's all. I got some friends. We get a kick outta watchin' everything fallin' apart.

ANN: Who? Who do you drive around with?

ED: It's a freak show. It's like watchin' people drown.

ANN: 'Cause it's not Rocky.

ED: Rocky's a freak.

ANN: It's not Charlie. Who?

ED: Friends.

ANN: I talked to your friends. They told me you been hanging out down by the piers, in those bars. Places where everything goes on. Is that true?

ED: What, I ain't got no friends no more?

ANN: What?

ED: I go to the docks. My father, my uncles, they all worked down there. You should see it now. It's going to shit. It's like a fuckin' swamp.

ANN: People on the street, they ain't got no dining room or living room. Ed, you got all those rooms.

ED: Brooklyn's going to shit.

ANN: Our marriage is going to shit. Listen, and try to hear me. I don't like it. If it's some other woman, I want it over right now and it's forgotten and forgiven.

ED: Ann, it's not another woman.

ANN: If you wanna play this game, I know the street too. I can stay out all night too.

ED: IT'S NOT ANOTHER WOMAN!

ANN: If it is, I'll get an annulment so fast you'll think I'm related to the Pope.

ED: Ann, you want to know the truth?

ANN: Yes!

ED: You are giving me the fuckin' biggest headache I ever had.

ANN: You want me to shut up?

ED: Yes.

ANN: Well I won't. Don't be scared.

ED: I'm not scared of fucking you.

ANN: I'm talkin' about the nightmares.

ED: I gotta go.

ANN: And the doctor said....

ED: Why don't the doctor come here and fuck you!

ANN: Oh my God.

ED: Don't you talk to God for me.

ANN: You don't touch my face. You don't play with my hair. You don't hold me.

ED: How am I supposed to touch you.... My hands don't stop shakin'.... Where's my aspirin.... My hands are all sticky.... Fuckin' coffee... You say I don't look at you.... I look at you.... What do you want from me? God, God, yeah right, that's a fuckin' joke.... You don't want a real man.... That's your problem. You're a weak little girl.... You can't handle me—you want a fag...you can't handle me...you want a fag like your father...a fag.... He's from Italy, right? (*As* ANN *goes to smack him*) Go ahead...I'm getting outta here. You're a sick violent pervert.

(*He leaves. Overlap to:*)

Scene Five

(ROCKY *is getting ready for his night. The place is a mess and dimly lit. At the door is* LINDA *in drenched clothes. She knocks.)*

ROCKY: She's not here! You hear me. Nobody home. You can bang all you want, but I'm not home. Hey, why don't you bang on your wife's door. Maybe if you were bangin' your wife, you wouldn't be bangin' on my door. Don't make me come out there. I'll shoot you. You hear me, I'm not home!

LINDA: And I'm not here!

(He opens the door.)

LINDA: Expectin' someone. Some construction worker with a pecker like a pinky. Figured out his wife's cigarette money went to smokin' your— You want breakfast?

ROCKY: —Are you crazy?

LINDA: That would explain a lot, wouldn't it?

ROCKY: Whatta you?... Come—

LINDA: I don't wanna get shot.

ROCKY: I thought you were the landlord.

LINDA: Where's the landlady?

ROCKY: Come in.

LINDA: Look, I'm.... Fuck this. I gotta go.

ROCKY: Come on, come in. There's a draft.

LINDA: When there's an earthquake, you're supposed to stand in the doorway. Funny, how we keep meetin' in doorways.

ROCKY: You want me to invite you in, is that it? "Would you like to come in?" Please! Before my landlord see you!

LINDA: Tell 'im I'm the cleaning lady.

ROCKY: You're soaked. What the hell— Dry off willya—

LINDA: This towel... It's dirty.

ROCKY: Use my shirt—it's clean. You're crazy crossin' the El at this hour.

LINDA: Funny, how the Berlin wall comes down, but that train track is still up.

ROCKY: It's how you get to the City.

LINDA: When the wall came down, they were sellin' pieces of it like paperweights? I'm gonna do that when the El comes down. Turn it into paperweights.

ROCKY: You're gonna catch...the draft. That's how you get sick.

LINDA: It's like a bomb went off in here.

ROCKY: I know where everything is.

LINDA: Wherever it lands. (She gets a chill.)

ROCKY: What, you fall in a puddle? You're gettin' the shakes. Is it rainin' out there?

LINDA: Some old guy on the corner, hosed me down. What the hell is that? What kinda people is that?

ROCKY: Who was it? Did you step on his lawn? Fuckin' guy is crazy about his lawn.

LINDA: I'm gonna go! I don't even know why I came over here. Just to see if I could.

ROCKY: Put somethin' on. Here.

LINDA: Pressed. You goin' out tonight? This is the only thing, including me, that ain't wrinkled in here.

ROCKY: I gotta straighten out, put things in order.

LINDA: So this is how I get to see the castle.

ROCKY: Your hat's on the bed, that's bad luck.

LINDA: I thought you didn't have a bed.

ROCKY: Yeah, I curl up on — it's a couch with no pillows.

LINDA: Are you lookin' at me? You want me, or my kids' lunch money?

ROCKY: No.

LINDA: So atomic boy. You got an appointment? Somebody comin' over with her laundry money. You oughta be in the Yellow Pages, under Lonely.

ROCKY: I don't go out for money?

LINDA: Oh, I'm sorry, for little jobs. For dinner. Breakfast in bed. You need an analyst.

ROCKY: What?

LINDA: What kinda suit is this?

ROCKY: Silk.

LINDA: I don't want it to get wet. It might get ruined. I don't know who else is gonna spray me.

ROCKY: It's off a fuckin' truck.

LINDA: A lotta trucks in your neighborhood. But nobody gets on 'em.

ROCKY: They don't make suits like they used to. Now it's all paste and staples, and.... It used to be canvas, and stitching. Nothin' is like it fuckin' used to be.

LINDA: You got a raincoat? In case that old guy still out there.

ROCKY: I'm sorry about that.

LINDA: The whole day's been strange. I got up this afternoon scared to death. I didn't know where I was. Like I was sleepin' in a strange bed—I miss—

ROCKY: —Me, too—

LINDA: —Shit—

ROCKY: —Sorry— You get the job?

LINDA: I'm gonna substitute a few days. But I gotta
take a test for full time. I gotta wait for the school year,
I'm close to twenty-seven and I gotta wait for school.
I oughta be a conductor, on that train. Go back and
forth from the city to Brooklyn.

ROCKY: If I had a teacher like you, maybe I woulda
went to college. How's the?

LINDA: —They're—

ROCKY: —Good. They still doin' their tables. Two times
two is?

LINDA: I gonna give my aunt her place back.

ROCKY: Where you goin'?

LINDA: The City.

ROCKY: Yeah?

LINDA: Friend of—

ROCKY: Nice. You're finally gettin' back.

LINDA: Yeah, wow, this is, I'll call you.

ROCKY: You look good. Really good.

LINDA: It's your suit. That radio play anything else?

ROCKY: That fuckin' thing. Somebody gave it to me.
The FM don't work. It only gets a couple of stations.
I never thought I'd like the old stuff. Sappy romantic.
You know. I never thought. I'll come see you in the—

LINDA: No you won't.

ROCKY: I got that book I borrowed. I don't know. I start
a book, I get a headache, I start it again, I get another
headache. The pictures, Italy is beautiful. It's like
completely different, then....

LINDA: Maybe it's your eyes. Why do you always
squint, when you look in the mirror?

ROCKY: I look better that way.

LINDA: 'Cause at first I figured, this guy, I don't know if he can see me. But now I see you just need to make sure you were still there.

ROCKY: I got glasses, but....

LINDA: Right.

ROCKY: Lemme get you home.

LINDA: You're gonna walk me home? We might get wet.

ROCKY: If somebody sees us, it's trouble, but....

LINDA: You could follow me home? I'll walk ten feet in front of you like an Arab, or is it sand nigger to you?

ROCKY: I could get us a car.

LINDA: It's only a couple of blocks.

ROCKY: I know how far it is. It's just you wearin' the suit. You look like a man. And crossin' the El...

LINDA: Oh, we're not gonna hold hands? And we're not gonna stop under the train tracks? With the rain comin' down? And we're not gonna kiss? That's too bad. That's the way the movie would end.

ROCKY: Look, it was good.... Let's just make it nice, so that when we run into each other it'll be like friends.... Fuck.

LINDA: Say fuck you. Say fuck it all. Jump! You'll land right on the platform. Whatta you gonna do now, light some firecrackers? What, you're gonna say something. I'm glad I could serve you. Check the black one off your list, killer. But next time you need a maid who spreads her legs, go down to the terminal and buy it like every other white boy. What? I like this suit. I'll wear your suit home, down the avenue, with my head up high. I'll wear it like a man should.

(Overlap to:)

Scene Six

(Lights up on ED. *He stares at the audience.* ROCKY *watches him. They are on the corner.)*

ROCKY: Is that you?

ED: Who the hell you think it is.

ROCKY: Maybe you're a ghost.

ED: Yeah, like *The Night of the Living Dead*?

ROCKY: Those were zombies.

ED: Same fuckin' difference. I saw you through the window at that fish restaurant.

ROCKY: Yeah, worked there for a day, cuttin' clams. I smelled like fish. You see anybody walkin' by? Dressed up and shit?

ED: Who?

ROCKY: Anybody?

ED: Hey, look, over here. There's a bee. In the candy store. Right on the other side a the window. The bee sees the street light. So it keeps slammin' into the glass to get out. It bounces off, hits the floor. Gets up and goes at it again. Stupid fuckin' bee.

ROCKY: *(Looks in)* Ed, that's a big fly.

ED: You come down to the corner anymore? I still do. Sometimes I just stand around all night, waitin'...for somethin'. You ever just wait? Sometimes I just wait for somethin' to happen. Or I just wait for anything. Like I pick up somethin' just to wait for it. Like I say, I'm waitin' for Sunday. Sunday comes, the next thing you know it's Monday.

ROCKY: Whatta you waitin' for now?

ED: My brother. Where ya been? I feel like I'm missin' my better half.

CHARLIE: *(Enters)* How's it hangin'?

ED: *(Grabs his crotch)* Sometimes it hits the floor.
Oooh, the sidewalk's cold.

ROCKY: Whatta you see?

CHARLIE: I don't see and I don't hear and I don't know.
I'm blind, deaf, and dumb. I'm like them three monkeys
in one.

ROCKY: Still goin' to the cage?

CHARLIE: Ain't been there for weeks.

ROCKY: You gotta keep hittin' homers if you wanna
keep seeing Yankee Stadium.

CHARLIE: Only thing I hit is the bottle.

ED: I ain't seen you since you hit on me for work.

CHARLIE: *(Looking into the candy store)* Rosie's retirin'.
Kids don't buy candy no more. I oughtta open a drug
store, and I don't mean aspirin.

ROCKY: Yeah, put up some mirrors.

CHARLIE: The pretty boys ain't so pretty no more.

ED: Hang out now. I'm dyin' here all alone. St. Charles,
bless me. *(He gets on his knees.)*

CHARLIE: Get up. I gotta go.

ED: You leave your balls at home tonight? You get it
every night. Hang out.

CHARLIE: Bullshit. She's like my old man's car.
When it's cold she won't turn over.

ED: *(Miming smacks)* Give her a couple. It warms 'em up.

CHARLIE: Maybe it'a shut her up. She's always
bitchin'.... She wants to go back to school. They give her
shit at work.

ED: Buy her a book.

ROCKY: It's like we been outta school forever.

ED: What she want with school anyways? She knows howda type.

CHARLIE: Fuckin' kid! The god-damn wailin'. I walk outta my house with a bell ringin' in my head.

ED: Buy the kid one a them.... Them things for dogs. A muzzle...

CHARLIE: I gotta get a family pack.

ROCKY: Ya bring the kid to the bar?... Can't hear yourself think over there. It's like a maternity ward.

CHARLIE: These days the father's the mother. How many are yours? I left you mine, with a note.

ROCKY: Very funny. But I am gettin' the cold shoulder.

CHARLIE: 'Cause word is you're bangin' a nigger.

ED: I see the brown under your fingernails.

CHARLIE: Real estate, it's all about real estate, man.

ROCKY: She's French. She's in the City. She's a model.

CHARLIE: And you go through the projects to get there?

ROCKY: I'm tired of Italian girls. They just lay around and make you beg for it.... Now French women—

ED: Eat a lot of fried chicken.

CHARLIE: Somebody saw a nigger leavin' your house, and he wasn't the mailman.

ROCKY: Yeah. Where? He was sellin' somethin'.

ED: Maybe Rocky's starting a basketball team.

ROCKY: You ever think about that guy? Remember?

CHARLIE: God-honest truth. I don't think about it.... One day though. I'm watchin' some cartoon on TV.... I don't know, some coyote is tryin' to blow up a bird, when all of a sudden I feel this shit climbin' up my neck.

ED: Maybe it was somethin' you ate....

CHARLIE: Yeah. Maybe somethin' I drank, too.

ED: Rocky, all I wanna know is, does she come like a white woman? Or does she scream like a chimp?

ROCKY: At least I'm fucking a girl.

ED: Hey, Sally's is packed every night with girls who still know how to have a good time. Those big tits, the makeup, them skin-tight dresses.

CHARLIE: You ever do stuff with them?

ED: I just watch 'em. You ever watch 'em? It's like slow. It's so slow you see it clear. I can't even remember what I had for breakfast, but I remember exactly how they move.

ROCKY: If I was fuckin' your wife, I wouldn't fuck around with the fags from Henry's.

CHARLIE: That's not saying much, since you'd fuck anything that stands still long enough.

ED: They want me. They want me so bad. I'm the strongest sonovabitch in this neighborhood. Feel that muscle. That muscle's younger than me.

ROCKY: Whatta you wanna do? Go chasin' spics and niggers your whole life. Go to the bar. Get drunk. Talk some shit. Beat somebody up.

ED: Yeah, Charlie, let's go beat somebody up.

ROCKY: Go home and beat up your wife like everybody else.

ED: She won't fight back.

ROCKY: Fuck, talkin' to you.

CHARLIE: At least he don't eat out old women for subway tokens.

ROCKY: Charlie, relax, you wanna go back to the bar. You just gotta get your swing back—You strike out. You get right back to the plate. I try hittin' homers all night.

CHARLIE: Yeah, well, I caught one.

ROCKY: What? You got laid?

CHARLIE: No, but I got fucked. I shoulda known. I can't even hold my kid. I'm scared of droppin' 'em all the time.

ROCKY: Good-lookin' kid. Looks like me.

CHARLIE: That's right.... I been staring in my shopping bag all night, and I can see it. I can see it in his two-timing eyes. He looks just like you.

ED: But Charlie, Rocky's better lookin' than you.

CHARLIE: That night while I'm doin' her she's mumblin' somethin' that took me two years to figure.

ROCKY: You used to hold your liquor.

ED: You wanna fuck Ann, too?

ROCKY: You're fucked up. The both a yous.

CHARLIE: She was mumblin' your name. You dumped in the park that night. I laid my life down for you...and now you walk around here tellin' everybody you're gonna be in Hollywood.

ROCKY: Yeah, I got charisma...so what?

CHARLIE: You fuck their wives and their mothers with your stories.... You're a motherfucker.... I left the kid at the bar for you. You gonna get 'im yourself.

ROCKY: Hey, I tell ya, he ain't my kid.

CHARLIE: I just borrowed 'im. You can have 'im back.

ROCKY: I never done nothin' with your wife. She ain't worth energy.

ED: The kid's a little dark. Maybe she fucked a mool. (*Excited*) You wanna go to the projects and find your wife's boyfriend? We'll break his head like it was an egg.

CHARLIE: HEY SHUT THE FUCK UP ABOUT HER! She's alright.

ROCKY: She's a whore Charlie. Face it. You screwed up, you fucked a whore and now you gotta pay. That's what prostitutes are all about.

ED: They're all whores. Slave to the member.
(He grabs his crotch.)

(CHARLIE pushes ROCKY.)

(ROCKY grabs ED by the arm.)

ED: Let's see who hits the softest. You go first.

ROCKY: I know this joke.

ED: It's no joke, it's a game.

ROCKY: I don't wanna play.

CHARLIE: The only thing you care about is your dick!

ROCKY: Charlie calm down. Let's go get a drink.

CHARLIE: I'M NOT THIRSTY! I ain't even hungry. I'm not nothin'!

ROCKY: We're all gonna die when the bomb hits anyways.

CHARLIE: SHE AIN'T A WHORE.

ROCKY: Come on, shit for brains. Go out and get laid. You just ain't realistic. Like this baseball. You put all your energy into it and you just ain't smart or good enough. You shoulda played football, somethin' with hittin'. You're twenty years old and you're still playin' little league.

CHARLIE: *(He pushes ROCKY again.)* Fuck you.

ROCKY: Stop pushing me.

ED: Hit me! It's a game.

ROCKY: Hit yourself!

ED: Why don't you hit me?

ROCKY: I got no reason!

CHARLIE: Who do you think you are? You walk around in your fancy suits like some big shot. You think you're better than me. Than us. Just 'cause you're fuckin' a nigger don't mean you're from the city. Dressed up and shit, just like that black guy, think who you are.

(CHARLIE *pushes him again.*)

ROCKY: Look, you're drunk and you're saying stupid things. Now go home, go see your wife.

CHARLIE: You ain't nothing but shit, Rocky. You're a coward, who don't got the balls to do anything except put a bag over some broad's face and fuck her for a buck. *(He pushes* ROCKY *again.)* I never saw you fight. *(Another push)*

ROCKY: You're on thin ice.

CHARLIE: I never saw you hit nobody.

(Another push)

ROCKY: Go play some ball. Go make believe it's Yankee Stadium. Get outta here.

CHARLIE: You're the whore. You ain't gonna be pretty no more.

(ROCKY *punches* CHARLIE *in the face.* CHARLIE *falls to the floor.* ROCKY *grabs his hand, in pain.*)

ROCKY: Now get the hell outta here you stupid drunk.

(CHARLIE *is still on the floor.*)

ED: Just hit me. It's a game. You hit him.

ROCKY: No!

ED: You don't hit me, I'll kill you.

CHARLIE: You killed me Rocky.

ROCKY: Yeah, yeah. And you kill me. We all kill each other. We all kill each other. We're killers.

CHARLIE: I'll take care of your kid. I rather the kid had a father than a penis with ears.

ED: Gimme a hug.

CHARLIE: Get the fuck off me you sick bastard.

ED: Hug your brother.

CHARLIE: Go hug your wife. Did you hear me? You crazy fuck. She's down at the bar looking for your ass.

ED: Whatya tell her?

CHARLIE: I told her to get me a job, you greedy fuck. *(He leaves.)*

ED: Where you goin', Paris or the projects?

ROCKY: I'm goin' home.

ED: You wanna remember the black guy? Let's play. I'll go first.

ROCKY: I'm not gonna hit you back. I don't wanna play.

(ED hits ROCKY.)

ED: FIGHT BACK. HIT ME BACK.

ROCKY: You're a fuckin' animal.

(ROCKY shakes his head "no". ED beats ROCKY up.)

ED: What are you lookin' at?

(ED beats ROCKY up, the way he beat the black man. ROCKY lays on the floor, bloody, possibly dead.)

CHARLIE: You sick bastard.

ED: I just want a hug. Rocky, my brother. Gimme a hug. I love you.

(ED picks ROCKY up and gives him a hug and a kiss.)

(Overlap to:)

Scene Seven

(Lights up on WENDY lying on the couch watching TV with an ice pack on her eye. CHARLIE walks in and also has an ice pack on his eye. WENDY sees him and stomps away. CHARLIE blasts the volume on the TV.)

WENDY: Turn that thing down.

CHARLIE: What?

WENDY: I said turn it down!

CHARLIE: I can't hear ya.

WENDY: *(Gets remote and turns off the TV)* I SAID TURN IT DOWN!

CHARLIE: Whatta ya crazy or somethin'? Don't ever touch the TV while I'm watchin'.

WENDY: Shut up! You stink of alcohol and it's late.

CHARLIE: This is my house and I do what I want.

WENDY: Be quiet will ya... Your eye is swollen.

CHARLIE: You finally noticed.

WENDY: It's kinda hard when you only got one eye yourself.

CHARLIE: I got into a fight with Rocky.

WENDY: Rocky?

CHARLIE: You said the kid was his.

WENDY: That's sweet.... But it's not.

CHARLIE: But you said—

WENDY: Ain't nothin' that ugly can be Rocky's.

CHARLIE: You fuck him?

WENDY: Never.

CHARLIE: You fuck Richie?

WENDY: How many times I gotta tell you?

CHARLIE: You fuck a black guy?

WENDY: Hey, I fucked some people but they was all Italian.

CHARLIE: You're crazy, you know that? You're real crazy. You make me get into a fight with one of my best friends. What you tryin' to do, kill me?

WENDY: Make you jealous. And you was.

CHARLIE: Crazy and stupid. Sometimes you are a real asshole.

WENDY: What you want, it ain't easy being cooped up in here all night. No friends and nothin' to do. Sometimes you get doubts and they make you do crazy things.... I need ya Charlie. I still wanna have fun.

CHARLIE: You had your fun.

WENDY: We both did.

CHARLIE: Now we pay for it, that's the rules of the game. You think I'm having fun, this ain't no Disneyland. I put down just enough booze to forget about tomorrow. Look, I don't know if I even wanna be married. Everything's happenin' so fast, I didn't even have time to think about it. It's like I'm being punished.

WENDY: You don't think I don't want the same things you do? I'm with you. Together we can make it work. What you expect me to do, raise the kids myself? He's half yours.

CHARLIE: You sure?

WENDY: I'm sure.

CHARLIE: I don't know. He just don't feel right in my arms. He's like a roast beef or somethin'. What kinda father am I? I don't even know how to hold 'em. Am I gonna show 'em how to play ball? One thing I love and I couldn't even do it right. But now...

WENDY: You left the kid at your mother's?

CHARLIE: Holy shit, the kid.

WENDY: Where is he?

CHARLIE: I left him at the bar.

WENDY: You were supposed to go to your mother's.

CHARLIE: Nah, it was baby night at the bar. Bring a baby and get free drinks. You know, mister moms... You shoulda seen him with the little blue ribbon on him. He looked like a champion. He won first.

WENDY: He did?

CHARLIE: Most likely to follow the drunkard steps of his father. Funny?

WENDY: If you don't get him, I'll kill you. I'll break every bone in your stupid little body. First, your mother tries to kill 'im with her food, and now you lose him at a bar, unfuckin' believable.

CHARLIE: Will you shut up about my mother.

WENDY: You didn't want 'im you shoulda told me. How did I ever marry you?

CHARLIE: Be quiet will ya. He's all right. Lotsa kids there. *(Picks up the phone and dials)* Nicky, it's Charlie. My kid there?... No, I don't wanna talk to him. He's in a bowlin' bag. Wendy, they got six kids in bowlin' bags there. *(Into phone)* He's wearing the blue ribbon. No it's not Rocky's kid, it's my kid.... I wrote the note. I put it on there.... Cross out "Rocky," put "Charlie." I'll be right over. Don't let anyone get him. And don't give him any drinks, you pusher you. *(He hangs up.)*

WENDY: You are the dumbest man I've ever met! *(She starts to get up.)*

CHARLIE: Whatta you doin'?

WENDY: I ain't sleepin' with you tonight.

CHARLIE: Where are you sleepin'?

WENDY: I'm sleepin' on the floor.

CHARLIE: Sleep on the couch.

WENDY: Don't tell me what to do.

CHARLIE: Do I gotta drag you?

(He's on top of her.)

WENDY: Leave me alone... Get the kid.

CHARLIE: I love you Wendy.

WENDY: If anything happens to that kid I'll kill you.

CHARLIE: Wendy, I love you. If anybody touches you or the kid, I'll run 'em over.

(He picks her up and holds her for a moment.)

WENDY: You forgot to turn on the TV.

CHARLIE: Where's the remote?

WENDY: Bring me to the table... Turn me around...

(She gets the remote and turns the TV back on. CHARLIE then lays her gently on the couch and puts the comforter on top of her.)

CHARLIE: Go to sleep baby.

(Overlap to:)

Scene Eight

(Lights up on ANN in her and ED's dining room. She is at the table, numb and shocked. ED comes staggering in, his shirt open. We can see spots of blood on his back)

ED: Ann, it's the dream. The fucking dream. It's always in my head. I close my eyes for a second and it's always there.

ANN: Was that a man or a woman? My God, the makeup, the wig.

ED: Why did you find me? How?

ANN: I'm the only fool in this whole neighborhood who doesn't know. I'm blind. I'm blind!

ED: I'm sorry.

ANN: All this time I'm thinking you're seeing another woman and it's a man. Why was he hitting you like that? Why??

ED: I shoulda killed her.

ANN: Him! Do you fuck them?

ED: No. They want me so bad but I don't.... I don't Ann.

ANN: Then what? You're friends? You hold hands?

ED: I hate 'em.

ANN: God damn you! GOD DAMN YOU!!

ED: I need it, don't you understand? I go crazy if I don't get it. I try to stay away. I just hadda get it knocked outta my system. It's good for you. My folks did it to me as a kid, it kept me in line. The belt was good for you.

ANN: It's my fault or somethin'.

ED: There's nothing wrong. It's over, I won't go back.

ANN: It's not right to get whipped like that.

ED: When you got temptation, you gotta fight it. Right, Ann?

ANN: No!

ED: When you sin, you repent. Right Ann? RIGHT???

ANN: NO!!! This is too much. It's too much!

ED: Ann, I won't go back! Just don't tell anyone.

ANN: No. God, maybe it's my fault. Maybe I did this to you. You don't want a kid is that it?

ED: I wanna be your husband.

ANN: You're dripping...what is.... That's blood. Oh my God Ed what did you do?? Look at that blood!

ED: It's nothing.

ANN: You're bleeding all over the place!

ED: I wanna have a kid. Let's do it now.

ANN: Stay away from me! Oh my God Ed what did you do??

ED: The dream Ann.

ANN: It's just a dream!!

ED: It don't feel like a dream. Like it ain't real no more.

ANN: You're sweatin' like a pig. *(He laughs.)* What's so funny?!

ED: Pigs don't sweat. People do.

ANN: You could die!!!

ED: Maybe I'll die. I don't die in the dream. When I fight that guy from the projects. When he hits me in the back with that bat, it don't hurt, it just burns on them giant scars. And the burnin' makes me feel better. Like we're even. But the part that don't make sense is the guy in the dream is dressed like a girl—Ann, I'm protecting you in the dream. It's you I'm keeping him away from. You and the neighborhood. That's why I kill 'im every time.

ANN: I'm leaving.

ED: Help me!

ANN: Help you? I'm the one who needs help now!

ED: Maybe they should get cleaned or else they'll get infected. Please, Ann! Please, Ann... Please Ann. Forgive me, Ann.

ANN: *(Pause)* God. I loved someone who looked like you. *(Goes into other room)* Where's the alcohol?

ED: I did it all for you!

ANN: Shit, where's the alcohol?

ED: If Rocky and Charlie were around, I'da killed that faggot who was hurting me.

ANN: *(Re-enters with rubbing alcohol)* This is gonna burn.

ED: We'da killed him. I love them guys. You don't understand me, the way they do. I love them. We're more than brothers, we're each other.

ANN: It's gonna hurt Ed.

ED: Forget and forgive...

ANN: ...And I wanna hurt you.

ED: DO IT ANN!

ANN: I hope this hurts you. I hope it kills you!
(She pours the alcohol.)

ED: They're burning Ann! Just like the dream!
They're burning, I knew they would! *(Turns around
and kisses her)* Do it again Ann.

ANN: No.

ED: Please Ann, like my lover!

ANN: Yes! *(Stares at him and then nods her head.
As she pours:)* Yes.

(Overlap to:)

Scene Nine

(Lights up on LINDA's *doorway.* ROCKY, *blood smeared,
comes in. He pauses for a moment and then starts knocking
at the door. The rumble of the train is heard.* ROCKY *knocks
louder.)*

ROCKY: LINDA. OPEN THIS DOOR! LINDA PLEASE
OPEN IT! LINDA PLEASE!

(A light is turned on. She appears.)

LINDA: Shut up before you wake the whole building.
They shoot you to go to sleep around here.

ROCKY: LET 'EM SHOOT. ANYBODY WANNA
SHOOT ME!? GO AHEAD, TAKE A SHOT AND GO
TO SLEEP. SHOOT THE WHITE BOY AND GO TO
SLEEP.

LINDA: Go home.

ROCKY: ANYBODY HURT YOU. I DON'T KNOW.
YOU WEARIN' THAT SUIT I STARTED THINKIN'.
THEY KILL YOU AROUND HERE FOR WEARIN' A
SUIT.

LINDA: You're gonna wake my kids.

ROCKY: You're gonna love me, if I have no eyes,
if I have no nose, if I have no lips, if I ain't pretty.

LINDA: If this is about your face. Are you drunk!?

ROCKY: Yeah, I'm high on life. You gonna kiss my face.
'Cause I got kisses all over my face. My friends love me
so much they kiss me. You're gonna kiss me too.

LINDA: I'm leaving.

ROCKY: I wanna come in an' kiss the kids.

LINDA: Are you kidding me?

ROCKY: I GOT A JOB!

LINDA: Yeah, where?

ROCKY: Waitin'. It's a hundred, sometimes a buck fifty a
night, cash, clean, under the table.

LINDA: I'm happy for you. That's what most pretty boys
do. Waitin' on tables. Flirtin' with old ladies. Take the
leftovers home.

ROCKY: And I got a friend who can rent me a place out
on the Island. What's wrong with the Island?

LINDA: They arrest you for bein' black out there.

ROCKY: They arrest you for being black everywhere.

LINDA: And what, I can sit around with the PTA,
watchin' talk shows and talkin' about what, busing?

ROCKY: A house. That's all anybody wants.

LINDA: Stop it! Stop that talk. It's not real.

ROCKY: IT'S A REAL HOUSE!

LINDA: I don't need a house, or a TV or a toaster, or any
other thing that falls off all the trucks drivin' in and out
of this neighborhood. I'm gettin' on one of those trucks.

ROCKY: I'm on my knees. I'm praying. God damn, look
through this keyhole and see me. *Will you marry me?*
(Pause) Will you marry me?

LINDA: What would your friends say at the wedding?

ROCKY: It'll be a real small wedding.

LINDA: I'm gonna open it now.

ROCKY: Linda, there's somethin' I gotta tell you.

LINDA: Put it on the table when you get in.

ROCKY: Sometimes, when we're goin' to that place, makin' love. Somethin' comes in my head. A couple a years back. This guy, a black guy, he comes 'round for a sandwich. I don't know, grilled cheese. Everybody on the corner, talkin' about girls, cars, how to make a million. And the next thing I know—like a fire goin' through a house. It's so fast it was like all at once.... They're kickin' him and hittin' him with a bat like his head was a baseball. And I heard it crack. He was drownin' in his own blood and I'm just watching.... I see it so real I hadda make it fake. It's the truth.

(LINDA *rubs the door.*)

ROCKY: Linda, I didn't hit 'im.

(LINDA *walks away.*)

ROCKY: You there, Linda, I didn't touch him.

(LINDA *stops.*)

ROCKY: I didn't do nothin'.

(LINDA *moves away.*)

ROCKY: I didn't have to tell ya!

LINDA: Yes you did, but I don't have to forgive you.

ROCKY: Life is short. The past is the past. Let's worry about us. When the bomb hits.... We're all gonna die anyways.

LINDA: The world's not gonna end with a bomb! It's gonna end with people like you standin' around, doin' nothin'!

(She starts to walks away.)

ROCKY: Come on Linda, open up. LINDA! OPEN THIS DOOR! LINDA PLEASE! OPEN IT! LINDA PLEASE!!! I love you....

(LINDA *walks away; she shuts off the lights.*)

ROCKY: Who we kiddin', we couldn't work.... You and me in the suburbs, no way. How could we live that lie. Picket fence, *Father Knows Best* bullshit....

(*He slides down the door in pain.*)

You think girls don't want me. You think I can't get someone to love me? I'M THE ONE WHO'S WHITE. (*He tries to light a cigarette and can't.*)

(*Overlap to:*)

EPILOGUE

(*The lights come up on the three women.*)

ANN: I got Ed a job at the church. Yeah, he cleans up after weddin's, funerals and baptisms. He works all the time, cleanin', polishin', washing the altar. I'm in the rectory most of the day, cooking somethin' for the priest, laundry, wife things. I play at Mass, but not too many people come anymore. When I was little, I remember seven o'clock Mass, Saturday night, that was full. Some kids broke in and tried to steal the chalice, and Ed caught 'em. I don't know how somebody could do a thing like that.

WENDY: Me and Charlie's anniversary. It was just us and the kid. Rosie used to say, "Nothin' ever changes ova here". It's kinda true and kinda not. The streets were music. Now the streets are dead, except for a few corners here and there. Some Sundays you walk around and you feel like you're in some western movie, like at high noon. All quiet like, you can hear the breeze blowin'. Dogs kinda limp by. At one time there was a hundred kids at the park watchin' the fireworks show

from Coney Island. Some nights I go up to the roof,
come summer, and watch the sky and remember.
Charlie, he sits in the car alot, he don't go nowhere,
it's like his office. The kids are startin' to talk now, I'm
tryin' to help, but it's fuckin' hard. I don't know, it feels
like somethin's over, but I don't know when it ended.

LINDA: I don't like to go to Brooklyn no more. Like
when you see it in a movie or something, you're like,
let's check it out, it's different. Once, I was out with the
people from work, and this guy who has a car, he says
I know the best Italian restaurant in the city. There's
always a guy who says things like that. So we cross the
bridge, and I'm headin' back. And in the restaurant,
I looked in through the kitchen door, and I swear I saw
Rocky, his face a little dented, a little beer belly, his hair
a mess, cuttin' clam after clam.

WENDY: Here's Frankie again. *(Sinatra sings "What
America Means To Me".)* That's the story. There ain't
no opera singin'. There ain't no pizza flyin'. There ain't
no mob guns shootin'. Just people. People tryin' to live
in their place.

ANN: Pleasant dreams.

LINDA: Goodnight.

(Curtain)